WE HAVE FOUND OUR LOVED ONES

When faced with chaos in the world or in your life read this book.

By Luther's Mouse

ISBN 9798365120297

We Have Found Our Loved Ones
Chapter I

Someone will challenge me, "You have no scientific answers. Retract your book!" I respond, "If I don't have better news for you than you have ever heard in your life, throw this book away. I apologize that you have wasted even the tiny price of this book. To prove who's right, and maybe it's you, come along and read."

Close your eyes. Open your eyes. I moved you to a funeral home, or you might actually be sitting in one right now. People sitting in a funeral home wonder, "What has become of my loved one?" or "What shall become of me?" or "How can I make it without my loved one?" or "Loved one, where art thou?" or "What sustains my loved one now?" or if you are a poet, "Distress to me for thee, my brother." —2 Samuel 1:26 Smith's Literal Translation. Close your eyes. Open your eyes. Now you are back. I did not keep you in the funeral home for more than a minute. That is because I am trying to be flippant about death like saints of old and present-day martyrs. This attitude was expressed on behalf of all the saints by St. Paul.

> For to me, to live is Christ and to die is gain. If I am to go on living in the body, this will mean fruitful labor for me. Yet what shall I choose? I do not know! I am torn between the two: I desire to depart and be with Christ, which is better by far; but it is more necessary for you that I remain in the body. – Philippians 1:21-24 NIV

St. Paul cared deeply about the people he ministered to, but he was neutral about going or staying. To get this right, I must be flippant also. I must either have faith and courage like they did, or maybe I could just pretend. I have endeavored to include solid answers for you in this book, scientific answers. I want to convey facts to you, wonderful facts, like the sweet words of Paul.

I wrote the following about a man.

> I am privileged to have known an excellent man named Richard R. In spite of the fact that he worked really hard for at least six decades, he found time to be a friendly, positive, loving person. He was a valued friend to all. This is the sign of a blessed man.
>
> It is a major event in heaven when the number of saints increases by just one. All the glory of the earth is pitiful compared to the smallest ceremonies of heaven. Each new saint is embarrassed. I am not worthy of this adulation, he says.

The saints all shout, "Worthy is the Lamb," who says, "Well done, Richard."

The endless sweet fellowship has now begun. Richard is reunited with dear friends and family he knew and with those he will begin to know. On earth he knew them by the dozens. In heaven he will know them by the billions, but he will know them in far deeper ways than by the mere earthly capabilities that he used to have.

Whenever you notice beauty in the sky, it is a reminder that the saints have gathered for such a reception and then have gone to their various pleasures leaving that sign behind. No wonder the yearning prayer is, "Thy will be done on earth as it is in heaven." No wonder the yearning is that earth become like heaven.

This is what I wrote, because this is what I felt that I knew about Richard R. I was not guilty of bilious flattery, though it may seem so. But I would not be surprised to learn that I was the only one to notice that Richard had a victorious life. What I have to impart to you is not that a victorious life earns heaven. Heaven cannot be earned, but that would not be a shock to us.

I do have surprising, shocking things to tell you. Most shocking of all is that the worst person you've ever heard of is still capable, upon repentance, of glory with the saints. This absurd view is fully proven by Mark 4:12.

> That seeing they may see, and not perceive; and hearing they may hear, and not understand; lest at any time they should be converted, and their sins should be forgiven them.

Where Jesus drives home a prophet's teaching.

> Make the heart of this people calloused; make their ears dull and close their eyes. Otherwise they might see with their eyes, hear with their ears, understand with their hearts, and turn and be healed. – Isaiah 6:10 NIV

And John the Baptist, in a similar vein, saw so much power in the repentance he preached that he wanted to restrict it.

> Then said he to the multitude that came forth to be baptized of him, O generation of vipers, who hath warned you to flee from the wrath to come? – Luke 3:7

Thus, we have it from prophets, our own consciences, and the Lord Himself that sinners should not be allowed to repent. All the preachers in history scream repent, but the Bible says, "Don't let them in on the secret; don't even tell them to repent."

Well, that is the bad part. But the good part, the pearl that quietly drops into a beggar's cup, is that the prophets and the Lord also reveal the treasure. The door to repentance is open.

Jonah and all prophets frowned at the same thing.

> God relented from the disaster that He had said He would bring upon them [Nineveh], and He did not do it.

> But it displeased Jonah exceedingly, and he became angry.
>
> So he prayed to the Lord, and said, "Ah, Lord, was not this what I said when I was still in my country? Therefore I fled previously to Tarshish; for I know that You are a gracious and merciful God, slow to anger and abundant in lovingkindness, One who relents from doing harm. – Jonah 3:10-4:2

And the testimony of a psalmist,

> If I regard iniquity in my heart, the Lord will not hear me: But verily God hath heard me; he hath attended to the voice of my prayer. Blessed be God, which hath not turned away my prayer, nor his mercy from me. – Psalm 66:18-20

Even in the simplest example of humans in the early world, a restriction was instituted against Adam and his descendants.

> And the LORD God said: 'Behold, the man is become as one of us, to know good and evil; and now, lest he put forth his hand, and take also of the tree of life, and eat, and live for ever.' He drove out the man; and He placed at the east of the garden of Eden the cherubim, and the flaming sword which turned every way, to keep the way to the tree of life.
> – Genesis 3:22-24 Jewish Pub. Soc. Tanakh 1917

The tree of life was protected against sinners because they were by no means worthy of its sweetness.

But greater than this prohibition was the word of salvation in Genesis 3:15.

> **And the Lord God said unto the serpent... I will put enmity between thee and the woman, and between thy seed and her seed; it shall bruise thy head, and thou shalt bruise his heel.**

Luther concludes,

> **This, therefore, is the text that made Adam and Eve alive and brought them back from death into the life which they had lost through sin.**
>
> *Luther, M. (1999, c1958). Vol. 1: Luther's works, vol. 1: Lectures on Genesis: Chapters 1-5 (J. J. Pelikan, H. C. Oswald & H. T. Lehmann, Ed.). Luther's Works (Ge 3:16). Saint Louis: Concordia Publishing House.*

The little clue, "her seed; it shall bruise thy head," when believed upon was enough. Faith only needs such a clue. Adam and Eve made their way to, not merely some tree, but to the true tree of life.

So, there it is, proven. Mockers call it "cheap grace." Beyond all doubt, cheap grace is a Bible teaching. And simultaneously, skepticism about repentance is also a Bible doctrine. It is a standing contradiction.

We do not know why repentance is allowed in the extreme case; the Lord knows why. We are curious about this limit, and this is a case where we are tempted to contradict the whole thing, including what was taught by Jesus Christ himself. But it is better instead to build a fence around this than to rebelliously trample on it. The explanation I offer is His will, referring to God's "secret will."

> **For he saith to Moses, I will have mercy on whom I will have mercy, and I will have compassion on whom I will have compassion. – Romans 9:15**

This kind of decision is thus reserved to God alone and is His secret. It is significant that Moses had just requested, "Please show me Your glory."— Exodus 33:18. Moses was also told, "You cannot see My face, for no one can see Me and live." We wonder about this limit also. Repentance is critically important and extreme, just as extreme as Moses' request. God's secret will determines the response to both requests. It could even be argued that true repentance and seeing the glory of God are one and the same.

The will of God is singular, but it has two aspects, the revealed will of God and the secret will of God. If God had no secret will, then God would be merely a mechanism; every action would be predictable. He is certainly not a mechanism; therefore, God has a secret will. He cannot really be predicted except to say that God's actions will be fully within the revealed will of God.

> **Surely the Lord GOD will do nothing, but he revealeth his secret unto his servants the prophets. – Amos 3:7**

Moses had been raised as a prince of Egypt, so he was literate. Some of those who fled Egypt with Moses knew writing also.

That, I think, was the second greatest treasure they brought out. (The greatest treasure was the Holy Seed, somewhere in Judah's descendants.) We are heavily indebted to every faithful copyist since then, or maybe earlier. We are similarly indebted to every faithful scribe, translator, and teacher. Likewise, solid interpretations don't fall from the trees either. With the help of angels and saints gone before, scholars have done their best for us. Floating on an ocean of doubt, we give thanks for our little boat, by which I mean the little that we know.

Even if we cannot read or write, our priests can teach us much about the will of God. If faithful, they would teach us the "received theology."

Having learned letters, we ourselves can read the Bible and many things. We develop bad interpretations, heresies, and monstrous theories. Rereading the received theology, we are humbly grateful to find rational interpretations and a fair amount of agreement about the revealed will of God.

By contrast, the secret will of God is not being revealed to us. The door is locked. We are supposed to pursue knowledge of God's will, ignoring barriers, even that one. This means we will slam up against it. Nevertheless Matthew 4:4 urges us on,

> **But he answered and said, It is written, Man shall not live by**

bread alone, but by every word that proceedeth out of the mouth of God.

And Deuteronomy 8:3,

And he humbled thee, and suffered thee to hunger, and fed thee with manna, which thou knewest not, neither did thy fathers know; that he might make thee know that man doth not live by bread only, but by every word that proceedeth out of the mouth of the LORD doth man live.

We will find good and satisfying answers, but eventually we hit the wall of that secret will. Along the way, we are fed spiritually, and I could even say there is a pot of gold at the end of the rainbow, “to those seeking Him He becometh a rewarder.”—Hebrews 11:6 Young's Literal Translation. It is important to note that this study does not claim to know any secrets but ferrets them out.

From time to time it may seem that his book is talking down to you. I apologize and offer this solution. Just imagine a mouse on the floor behind a tiny pulpit squeaking out a sermon right up to you. The mouse “enforces” his point, “Grace!” Squeaking even more, “Grace, you dear idiot. Don’t you get it?” It is a good sermon even though it is proud and condescending. But didn’t the mouse depart from the Bible? Actually, no.

The bodily life I now live, I live believing in the Son of God, who loved me and sacrificed himself for me. Consequently,

> I refuse to stultify the grace of God by reverting to the Law. O you dear idiots of Galatia. – Galatians 2:21-3:1
>
> *J.B. Phillips New Testament by using BibleGateway.*

The mouse has spoken well, and it is straight from the Bible. Let's assume that the little mouse is attempting to talk down to you. Who cares?

The biggest stumbling block about grace is accountability. Certainly, we should insist on accountability. In fact, someone may slam the table and scream down to the mouse, "How about accountability?" The mouse says,

> The amount of grace poured on someone determines everything good about them, achievements, good influence, love, virtue, holiness, talents, everything and, yes, accountability. Grace erases everything bad about them. Some will object.
>
> Ha! Ha! Ha! I repeat. The supply of grace is the most powerful thing on earth or in heaven, it determines everything. Grace overcomes all other powers. How much grace can you handle? Ready or not, here it comes. "O grave, where is thy sting?" includes "O accountability, where is thy sting?" Nothing can stand against Jesus "blotting out the handwriting of ordinances that was against us, which was contrary to us, and took it out of the way, nailing it to his cross." – Colossians 2:14

So much for accountability. Accountability is good. But here is what this teaches, accountability loses its final battle. Jesus holds all accountability within himself.

Squeaketh the mouse, “Cheap grace is cheapy cheap, cheap. Get it?”

I know it seems that grace makes me appear less than serious. My response if, “How serious are the blessed supposed to be?” Consider this, “I laugh at my enemies; how joyful I am because God has helped me!”— 1 Samuel 2:1 (it’s in the Good News Translation of Hannah’s prayer). We, like her (Samuel’s mother), can find our way through difficulties in such a way that it seems that we never had any. Difficulties, what difficulties? The blessing of not being downcast is not always with us, of course. But Hannah speaks nothing of sorrow, depression, or malaise, even though she had experienced them. She loves to say, “How joyful I am.” She found joy, unexpected joy, having passed through challenges. “I laugh at my enemies,” indicates that she had the joy while she was challenged. While she was passing through difficulties, the joy strengthened her. This is a personal power explained in many places, especially Nehemiah 8:10, “The joy of the LORD is your strength.” That strength is a great help to “find grace to help in time of need.”— Hebrews 4:16.

I have dealt with the blessed, but what about the desperate, the oppressed, the despised, the rejected, the unjustly condemned to death, and the martyred? In the Middle Ages a term arose in the Church that summarized burdens, tolerable or not. The term is, "the holy cross." This habitual term was fully wise and correct.

Squeaketh the mouse, "It did not refer to their stupid physical relics which they adored in those times. They were duped by charlatans and loved it."

No, it applied to most Christians who individually suffered for their faith as Christ set forth.

> Then Jesus said to His disciples, "If anyone desires to come after Me, let him deny himself, and take up his cross, and follow Me." – Matthew 16:24 NKJV

We have the term, "a cross to bear," which means the same as this particular meaning of "the holy cross," and it has the advantage that it is not a confusing term. It could be useful to combine these to produce an unmistakable term, "the holy cross, meaning a cross to bear."

Luther offers insight on the holy cross, meaning a cross to bear.

> When faith begins, God does not forsake it; He lays the holy cross on our backs to strengthen us and to make faith powerful in us.
>
> *(((Luther, M. (1999, c1967). Vol. 30: Luther's works, vol. 30: The Catholic*

Epistles (J. J. Pelikan, H. C. Oswald & H. T. Lehmann, Ed.). Luther's Works (1 Pe 4:13). Saint Louis: Concordia Publishing House.)))

And,

> The truly Christian life goes along in faith, serves everybody through love, and bears the holy cross. This is the true color, adornment, treasure, and honor of the Christian Church.
>
> *(((Martin Luther, Luther's Works, Vol. 30: The Catholic Epistles, ed. Jaroslav Jan Pelikan, Hilton C. Oswald, and Helmut T. Lehmann, vol. 30 (Saint Louis: Concordia Publishing House, 1999), 182.)))*

Interestingly, a long face does not seem to be the Christian way, neither by command, "Be of good cheer; I have overcome the world."—John 16:33. Nor by the overwhelming optimism gushing from Christianity, even though it is the most persecuted religion on earth. Here is Luther's paraphrase.

> Christ says: To remain cheerful in the midst of all this, and to ward off defeat, remember only that I am the real Savior and God, and rely on Me; then you will encounter the true God and experience My omnipotent power and might.
>
> *(((Martin Luther, Luther's Works, Vol. 24: Sermons on the Gospel of St. John: Chapters 14-16, ed. Jaroslav Jan Pelikan, Hilton C. Oswald, and Helmut T. Lehmann, vol. 24 (Saint Louis: Concordia Publishing House, 1999), 25.)))*

Back to our quest.

To find our departed loved ones, to really find them, in the same sense as finding the North Star or the Big Dipper, we look to the GOD who is everywhere all the time.

"Wait," someone will say, "who said there is a god? Be logical. Be scientific."

Very well. Suppose I say, "You were told or should have been told that geometry is everywhere all the time." No one will say, "Who said that there is geometry?" We readily accept that there is geometry. Suppose we know plane and solid geometry at a high school level. Geometry is a very powerful tool. The definitions, principles, and rules are of value. But the treasure is that in geometry we have experienced discovery. The student performs proofs, even of geometry itself. Any B-student proves every theorem and builds up knowledge in the form of a procedure for solving problems and gaining more knowledge. Geometry, then, exists as a tool that we may try anywhere for any purpose. To find our loved ones who have departed, the pathway must be easy, no more difficult than geometry.

I, as I search for our friends, must follow a procedure as rational as I can make it. I will try to cling to geometry, to the science of physics, and to another severe limit. I choose to be limited to statements made in the Bible. This is a useful philosophical constraint, whether or not one believes the Bible. There is no choice in one thing; my quest must reach beyond where we, as mortals, can go or observe. The imagination is ready; we can do this.

I am about to display before you some things about heaven that you will want to know. I have no access to secret knowledge, but general knowledge will be sufficient for us.

And I pursue this quest, believing in my God; you, however, do not need to believe. It is fine if you disbelieve, fine if you mock, and fine if you laugh at my rambling. I urge you to never suspend disbelief. Don't even assume you are reading a credible source. If an angel or devil whispers something into my ear, to lead me well or to lead me astray, I won't know it. I will not know the source. I will just think that those thoughts are mine and thereby be wonderfully or else be stupidly influenced. So, watch out.

Squeaketh the mouse, "Get on with it, man."

We have now had the necessary safety briefing. We are now set to travel. (Yes, we are going to heaven in this little book.) So, I will start again.

We Have Found Our Loved Ones
Chapter II

GOD is everywhere all the time. This applies to any volume, whether to the earth, the solar system, the galaxy, the universe or even to a volume greater than the universe. In my opinion, we should not assume there could be a limit.

About this word, universe, let's try to create a sound. Start with the first syllable of "ooze" or "oolong tea," the word "ran," a long "o," put an "s" on the end, and intensely accent the last syllable. We have created a sound that is the pronunciation of "ouranos," a Greek word. Ouranos accidently sounds like universe; if, that is, the speaker has a mouth full of ice cubes—Ha, Ha. I think that similarity of sound is mere chance, but the word itself actually does mean "universe." Again, you can't make this up! Ouranos is also divine, it is a word that is also the name of a god, the Greek god of the sky. That god was known to the Romans as Uranus. We have given that name to the seventh planet from the Sun, the planet Uranus.

Why do I care? This entire study is headed for a revealing Bible verse where Jesus says, "ouranos," translated as heaven. Ouranos, the word not the god, therefore lasts forever. Imagine this, heaven and earth will pass away, but the words for them will not. Matthew 24:35 "Heaven and earth will pass away, but my words will never pass away." We are stuck with the oldest manuscript being in Greek. That is our gospel of Matthew, period. We do not, however, know what language Jesus was actually speaking. Greek is unlikely, even though this connection points to it. Or, I suppose that Greek was prepared for the Gospel of Matthew to fit into it.

(((According to https://tyndalehouse.com/explore/articles/did-jesus-speak-greek/ Jesus had extensive exposure to Greek, especially in Egypt.)))

Squeaketh the mouse, "I'm not buying Greek."

That was strange, but here is a word we know. Our teacher is the great and beloved agnostic, Carl Sagan, on his TV show, *Cosmos*.

> Cosmos is a Greek word for the order of the universe. It is, in a way, the opposite of Chaos. It implies the deep interconnectedness of all things. It conveys awe for the intricate and subtle way in which the universe is put together.

Cosmos occurs 186 times in the New Testament, whereas ouranos occurs 278 times. These are important words. Sagan correctly explains their relationship in our current usage, but there has been a reversal. At this time, Cosmos is sometimes greater than Universe, always on a par with it. In the New Testament, however, "cosmos" is translated as "world," whereas "ouranos" is translated as heaven, heavens, air, and sky. I have no choice but to follow the severe limit that I have chosen, those statements made in the Bible. I must use ouranos, that is, universe. When Jesus said, "ouranos," should I have said, "Lord, you gotta use cosmos"?

No matter what volume we imagine for the universe, GOD is greater because GOD transcends His creation. This is a spiritual as well as a physical statement. Let us look at why physical size matters. Let's ask ourselves what the point of geometry is in this discussion, and what, if anything, do size and geometry reveal?

No entity, not even the whole universe, can exceed GOD. By this we know something about both Creator and creation. GOD is larger than any number in any dimension we can imagine, a unique property of GOD. Nothing within our thoughts, including size, number, might, beauty, wisdom, love, excellence, good pleasure, or wonder can surpass GOD. No matter how far we ride in our imaginations, giving them free rein, GOD's reality exceeds those thoughts.

Squeaketh the mouse, "Don't make me puke!"

Now, we need terminology. If you read in a novel or magazine, "the omnipresence of the secret police" or "the ubiquitous street vendors," you are reading a joke, or a hyperbole, or a fact that requires exaggeration to help you get the writer's point. Exaggerations in literature take you to the feeling itself. These hyperboles are useful, but they cannot move you to the geometric limit. They transport you in a metaphorical sense, but they cannot take you all the way to the literal encapsulation of the universe. We cannot implement a thought experiment in our minds of the size of the universe. Nevertheless, these are the terms we need. "Omnipresence" means "present at all places all the time," and so does "ubiquity." These terms coincide. Even if some little distinction could be made, I choose to use them interchangeably. Only GOD could satisfy the full article of these terms. (You might insist that space itself satisfies them. We will address that issue later.)

But what if we resist? As the obstinate folk we truly are, let's all recite from "Invictus" by William Ernest Henley, "I am the master of my fate; I am the captain of my soul." Do you feel better now? I do. If we follow Invictus, we say, "I cannot be inside of any god! I would not have the invincible free will that I insist on having." We at first would totally resist the omnipresence and ubiquity of God—even if we believed in God. But suppose we hesitate? Suppose we are wise enough not to blurt out our rebellion. How can we resolve this? The Bible has answers.

Antiubiquitarianism, anyone? In my opinion no one is required to believe in ubiquity. But railing against ubiquity is another matter. It has raised divine anger. Let us resolve—by all means—to be on the right side of such an issue.

Consider First Kings, Chapter 20. In an effort to conquer, sack, and humiliate Israel, Syria's leader, Ben-hadad, put together an enormous army by allying with 32 kings. They boasted to Israel, "Your silver and gold are mine, and the best of your wives and children are mine." In the first battle, the Syrians were humiliated by the small Israelite army, which had received prophetic direction. To attack again next year, Ben-hadad needed an excuse for a horrible loss and a new plan.

> And the servants of the king of Syria said unto him, their gods are gods of the hills; therefore they were stronger than we; but let us fight against them in the plain, and surely we shall be stronger than they. – I Kings 20:23

Ben-hadad embraced this geometric insult to Israel's God, dooming himself to another complete disaster. A prophet confirmed that God's anger was because of what Ben-hadad and the Syrians were saying,

> Thus saith the Lord, Because the Syrians have said, The Lord

> **is God of the hills, but he is not God of the valleys, therefore will I deliver all this great multitude into thine hand, and ye shall know that I am the Lord. – I Kings 20:28**

Why would God care what those pagans were saying? Ben-hadad's name meant son of the god Hadad. So, a supposed son of a god said of the Hebrews' God, "He is not god of the valleys." We are solving a riddle, and this is a tell. If the son of God, the Messiah, will come later teaching ubiquity, a strong reaction could be expected. But how forceful should that reaction be?

God starts punishing because of this slogan, and He keeps on punishing. The stupid slogan, "He is not god of the valleys," was answered with an enemy army being defeated the second time. That makes sense.

So, is the story over? Nope. It's just started. God still pursues. Get this. God decreed that Ben-hadad was "appointed to utter destruction." Today we might say this is nearly a war crime. The death penalty seems to be too great a punishment for a slogan, but that was not the end of it. The next step is truly strange; punishment also fell on the people of God. At this point, Israel meant the northern kingdom, not Judah. The king of Israel and his whole kingdom were judged severely for sparing and making a treaty with Ben-hadad. Verse 42 reads,

> **Thus saith the LORD, Because thou hast let go out of thy**

hand a man whom I appointed to utter destruction, therefore thy life shall go for his life, and thy people for his people.

This doom eventually happened, causing the northern kingdom to be cast out, to become the "Lost Tribes." Therefore, God's repudiation of "He is not god of the valleys" simply must be important.

My interpretation is that this is a prophecy, which means that all, and I mean all, theologies that do not insist on God's ubiquity will eventually go out of existence. Will whole denominations go away like the Lost Tribes? Let us hope they will embrace ubiquity.

Squeaketh the mouse, "Sayonara to the lost tribes."

Let's just conclude: God does not want us to mock His ubiquity. This certainly dispenses with Antiubiquitarianism. Next, let us allow ourselves to ponder ubiquity and its deep consequences.

We Have Found Our Loved Ones
Chapter III

Someone estimates the universe has a span of 93 billion light years. If so, then GOD is larger than that. How do I know? No size or number is His equal. An objection is, “You should not use geometry this way. Geometry has nothing to do with theology.” My response is, “Wrong and wrong.” If God is God, He is certainly geometrically God as well. No geometry, no matter how large, minute, intricate, or complex is any challenge to GOD. We should use geometry wherever we randomly step, subjecting even God to our gaze. (Ha Ha!) However, a lot of people, especially pious people, resist this kind of reasoning. This grand speculation about things far away, can it find the loved ones who have passed from us or even the very saints? Stay tuned.

If GOD is everywhere, He is here. Here means here, right where you are, right now. As strange as it may sound, St. Paul emphasized that we ourselves are inside God, "For in him we live, and move, and have our being," or "for in Him we live, and move, and are" — Acts 17:28. That is where we are; there is nowhere else to be. You'll get used to it. He is simultaneously here and 93 billion light years away; near and far are the same with Him. With gods, size matters. Geometrically, there can only be one such GOD within Whom are all things. Only one God can have this property of omnipresence or ubiquity.

Let us consider how God reveals His nearness to us.

We Have Found Our Loved Ones
Chapter IV

Consider this statement: "To my knowledge, Lutheranism is the only theological tradition committed to ubiquitarianism." I found it on the internet. The author is unidentified.

I wish it were false because I want ubiquity to be well known and well regarded. Alas, it is not. We need a much wider acceptance than just you, me, and the Lutherans. I want the idea of ubiquity to be ubiquitous. And I think I have just shown that it shall be, if the story of Ben-hadad is a prophecy. Similarly, omnipresence is not well known, but it should be. It is seldom, if ever, the subject of preaching, even by those who believe it. Someday, when the prophecy comes to pass, ubiquity will be the consensus throughout the monotheistic religions. The main application of it historically has been in Christianity, specifically the Lutheran view of the Eucharist, that is, the bread and the wine.

We are working our way to understanding the extreme nearness of God. We would be contradicting ubiquity if we supposed that a spirit comes and unites with the bread, i.e., consubstantiation. To us, God is already present. The location of, geometrically or in any other sense, any Persons of the Godhead, is properly mystical, beyond our knowledge, and always perfect. If Jesus states, "This is my body," no movement is required for it to be fact. We would be as stupid as Ben-hadad if we were to think Jesus cannot be wherever he says. So, applying Occam's razor, ubiquity wins because it is simpler than either consubstantiation or transubstantiation. More clarity is needed, however, as to why consubstantiation is not correct.

Squeaketh the mouse, "Sayonara to Ben-hadad."

We Have Found Our Loved Ones
Chapter V

I, personally, do not like the term "consubstantiation" because one of its meanings is "a spirit comes and unites with the bread." Someone hastily called that "Lutheran." Unfortunately, this stuck. They use it in the definition: "The doctrine, especially in Lutheran belief, that the substance of the bread and wine coexists with the body and blood of Christ in the Eucharist." Coexist is different and better than "a spirit comes and unites with the bread."

What did Luther himself believe?

> Even if nothing but bread and wine were present in the Supper, and yet I tried, simply for my own satisfaction, to express the thought that Christ's body is in the bread, I still could not say anything in a more certain, simpler, and clearer way than, "Take, eat, this is my body." For if the text read, "Take, eat, in the bread is my body," or, "With the bread is my body," or, "Under the bread is my body," it would immediately begin to rain, hail, and snow a storm of fanatics crying, "You see! do you hear that? Christ does not say, 'This bread

> is my body,' but, 'In the bread, or with the bread, or under the bread is my body!' " And they would cry, "Oh, how gladly would we believe if he had said, 'This is my body'; this would have been distinct and clear. But he actually says, "In the bread, with the bread, under the bread, so it does not follow that his body is present." Thus a thousand evasions and glosses would have been devised over the words "in, with, and under," no doubt with greater plausibility and less chance of stopping it than now.
>
> *(((Martin Luther, Luther's Works, Vol. 37: Word and Sacrament III, ed. Jaroslav Jan Pelikan, Hilton C. Oswald, and Helmut T. Lehmann, vol. 37 (Philadelphia: Fortress Press, 1999), 306.)))*

There are two important things in this quote, (1) Luther saw a simple, clear way to understand, "Take, eat, this is my body," and (2) Luther did not invent or like, "in, with, and under."

What do Lutherans actually believe? Lacking the knowledge of ubiquity provided here, Lutherans struggle. The most official translation of the Augsburg Confession, Article 10. Lord's Supper has,

> Our churches teach that the body and blood of Christ are truly present and are distributed to those who eat in the Supper of the Lord. They disapprove of those who teach otherwise.
>
> *(((Tappert, T. G. (2000, c1959). The Augsburg Confession: Translated from the Latin (The Confession of Faith: 2, X-, 2). Philadelphia: Fortress Press.)))*

But according to "Augsburg Confession" From Wikipedia, Lutherans believe,

Lutherans believe that Christ's body and blood is truly present in, with, and under the bread and wine of the sacrament and reject those that teach otherwise. – Article 10

"In, with, and under" must have been an early insertion since Luther himself rejected it. We will find it useful, without believing it.

Focus on "comes and unites" from consubstantiation (this includes a change) versus "in, with, and under" (this does not imply a change). We do not say the sun, moon, and stars coexist with space; we say they are "in" space. How about, "the sun, moon, and stars are in, with, and under God?" Yes, this is a good restatement of ubiquity. No spirit comes to unite with the sun, moon, and stars. They were created inside of GOD; they remain there. They can change, be blown to bits, glow hotter, turn cold, or whatever. It all happens inside of God; that does is not change, and that is the point.

Consubstantiation is wrong for the sun, moon, stars, and wrong for the Eucharist. The word "consubstantiation," therefore, should be avoided because it leads to misunderstanding. Better to say "in, with, and under." We got rid of consubstantiation with in, with, and under. Later we will get rid of in, with, and under by applying ubiquity and the Trinity.

We have now found the official meeting of God and man. It is the true understanding of the extreme nearness of God. We have solved this riddle, but ubiquitarians are not alone in comprehending it.

According to Luther, Christians tend to get this correct, "The believer approached the sacrament in faith—not faith in the ubiquity of the body of Christ but faith in the promising God" — Martin L. (Vol. 37, Page 156). No matter how enthused I am about the doctrine of ubiquity, it is just a helper. Christians do not actually need it; faith is what prevails. It is important to note that each time any communicant eats the bread and drinks the wine, whether in mystical reverence or believing in transubstantiation, consubstantiation, or the understanding we have just derived from ubiquity—all agree. Virtually all groups look at this matter in their own unique way, but a unity in this diversity is possible. It is my conclusion that **instead of dividing peoples we can now combine peoples**.

If we add up the Christian groups believing in the "Real Presence" of Christ in the communion elements at the moment of receiving them, it is a majority of Christians who ever lived as well as the majority of Christians alive today. These believers subscribe to Roman Catholicism, Eastern Orthodoxy, Oriental Orthodoxy, the Church of the East, the Moravian Church, Lutheranism, Anglicanism, Reformed Christianity, even Methodism in England (but not Methodism in America). Real Presence is not, therefore, against the prevailing view; it is the prevailing view. There is, however, much dissent—shrill dissent. But dissenters, no matter how sure they are of themselves, are just a minority. "Real Presence" may at first seem odd, especially because the dissenters are loud, shrill, and gushing with authority. We are agreeing to Real Presence and rushing onward.

(((Luther, M. (1999, c1961). Vol. 37: Luther's works, vol. 37: Word and Sacrament III (J. J. Pelikan, H. C. Oswald & H. T. Lehmann, Ed.). Luther's Works (Vol. 37, Page 156). Philadelphia: Fortress Press.)))

(((The list was developed from "Real Presence of Christ in the Eucharist" in Wikipedia.

https://en.wikipedia.org/wiki/Real_presence_of_Christ_in_the_Eucharist)))

At this point, what do we know? We understand the official meeting of God with man in its most legitimate sense, which is also its intimate form, holy communion, the Eucharist. God is already and always within. It is we who change. In the Eucharist He is announced to us, touching us, touched by us, and known by us

We have arrived at an eternal mystery. I do not say that we have solved the mystery of divine love and our nearness to God. We have arrived at the main activity we will enjoy for the rest of eternity, the act of discovering the love of God. We explored how God reveals His nearness to us in our present mortal state. I am not capable of knowing the love, glory, or sweet satisfaction of the heavenly state. We end here this part of the discussion.

We Have Found Our Loved Ones

Chapter VI

I will not be treating in detail the many mysteries that ubiquity solves concerning the explanation of those Bible miracles that take place in circumstances of (1) at a long distance, or (2) throughout a large area, or (3) throughout a large volume. Ubiquity solves the geometry. Examples are:

1. Creation (kind of a big example);
2. The sourcing of the universal basic morality that appears on its own in distant peoples (kind of a big example);
3. The fire from heaven that destroyed Sodom;
4. Moses' rod/serpent and its might;
5. The plagues of Egypt;
6. Crossing the Red Sea;
7. The doom of Pharoah's re-enslavement army in the Red Sea;
8. Moses' brass serpent on a pole that cured snake bite instantly from a distance when the afflicted merely looked at it;

9. Tthe manna from heaven;

10. Quail at dusk with manna in the morning;

11. Aaron's rod that budded;

12. Tthe Earth swallowing up the rebellious sons of Korah;

13. The sudden stoppings of rivers for Joshua's priests so the army could cross over to Jericho over a river in flood, similarly for Elijah, and similarly for Elisha;

14. Jonah's ocean cruise (both above and below the surface of the sea) and how the sea was suddenly calm;

15. The little foxes of Samson;

16. Gideon's fleece that was miraculous in opposite directions;

17. Daniel in the lions' den;

18. The three Hebrew children and a mysterious fourth – like a son of the gods – in the fiery furnace which in no way harmed them but killed others;

19. A long severe drought at the word of Elijah and a sudden, mighty rain at the word of the Lord;

20. Virgin Birth;

21. Turning water into wine;

22. Jesus easily calming a storm;

23. Jesus and Peter walking on water;

24. Jesus' miracle of the loaves and fishes;

25. Jesus' healings at a distance;

26. How that virtue flowed from Jesus to heal a woman that he did not even see, and why he felt it;

27. How on the road to Emmaus, the hearts of the disciples

burned as they talked with a man who turned out to be the Lord;

28. Philip suddenly snatched to another place;
29. Just the right intensity of earthquake releasing Paul and Silas but harming no one;
30. And St. Paul's healing hankies.

All the healings in the Bible would be listed. Number 8 could be linear; 11, 16, 20, and 27 are small; 15 and 23 are areas. The remainder of this list, more than three-fourths of them, require ubiquity in volumes. Alternatively, volume would work in every case. The entire list, even the tiny Virgin Birth, smaller than the size of one of Mary's eggs, could be done by volume. Applying Occam's razor, I can state, "All miracles are volumetric," because it provides the simplest theory. And, think about it, the smallest is greater than the largest, because Virgin Birth is more important than the entire universe. The volumetric attribute testifies to ubiquity.

I think you can see that Bible miracles testify to ubiquity. This is especially true of healings. There is no healing in the Bible where surgery (reaching into the body) was used. Touching is about as far as it goes; and touching seems optional. But inside the body is where healing would have to happen. So healing is always at some distance but simultaneously at no distance, necessitating ubiquity. Each healing requires that God work invisibly inside the afflicted body part. For instance, in 2 Kings 5:1-19, Elisha avoided contact with the afflicted Naaman. Naaman was exasperated. He was at a loss to know why he could not even meet the prophet. We, of course, know why.

And now for faith healing in the present day. I have seen more than a few faith healers, and I have seen them up close. They were of the charismatic, Protestant kind. I thought I observed that people were blessed by seeking faith healing. In retrospect, the concept of "safe harbor" is a far better explanation; I will explain later. I bring up faith healing to state that in Bible miracles and healings, God testifies to something. If I suspected that anything was valid in the work of faith healers I have seen, I would take this opportunity to tell you. I don't suppose there was anything to which God wanted to bear witness.

Squeaketh the mouse, "I am getting in the prayer line, I need a Mercedes."

If a faith healer, a medium, or even a priest, were to prophesy something about our departed friends, should we believe it?

I say no—especially about "purgatory." Have you been told your loved one is in purgatory? Remember Luther's famous quip, "As soon as a coin in the coffer rings, the soul from purgatory springs." He accused John Tetzel as actually saying this to sell indulgences. Tetzel denied saying that, but in essence he was selling on that presumption. I will prove later that no cleric, preacher, priest, bishop, or pope knows the disposition of your loved one in the hereafter. You should and might well ask of me, "Aren't you telling us something about the dead?" My answer is, "Yes, but indirectly. I am teaching about God. That knowledge reveals our loved ones. I have nothing else to reveal."

(((A blog on bloggers.com called, "Beggars All Reformation & Apologetics," claims Tetzel denied it, but he certainly taught its sentiment.

https://beggarsallreformation.blogspot.com/2012/01/did-tetzel-really-say-as-soon-as-coin.html)))

We are ready to resume our quest. We are expert in ubiquity, but what does it reveal about our quest for loved ones departed? To pursue this knowledge, we now must ride our imaginations on into heaven. Dare we?

We Have Found Our Loved Ones
Chapter VII

Yes, we dare, and it is now time to do that. Thanks for staying with me this far. We now go to my new theory.

Here is how ubiquity helps. Ubiquity allows for a theory, one we will find is necessary, that there are two speeds. Two speeds?—Allow me to explain.

Squeaketh the mouse, "I never exceed 110."

The "first speed" is subject to those limits imposed upon the universe. It can be measured. The first speed is already understood because such speeds have been observed for quite a while now. Our science of physics finds, empirically, that the speed of light is our speed limit. Possible speeds might even be a little more than the speed of light but not a lot more. So, let us freely define the first speed as the range of speeds from zero to the speed of light. The first speed can be fast, quite fast in fact. But if we were trying to match Bible descriptions—is the first speed fast enough?

No. That speed is way too slow for the following statement, "they shall gather together… from one end of heaven [ouranos] to the other" (Mark 13:27 or Matt. 24:31, confirmed by Deut. 4:32; more later.) The point is that the gathering happens, or many gatherings happen, and travel to a gathering is necessary. Now, apply the maximum first speed, the speed of light. Is that speed fast enough?

Again, no. To us, the speed of light is fast, so fast that we can never attain it. And yet at that speed limit a gathering would take 93 billion years to assemble. The speed of light is a theological failure. Theology is not a failure, but a far greater speed than light speed is indicated.

Squeaketh the mouse, "OK, you got me worried."

Somehow, there must be a second speed. Not to worry. Revelation 5:4 treats the issue of a locked theological treasure, "And I wept much, because no man was found worthy to open and to read the book, neither to look thereon." Reading on, Christ has prevailed (past tense in Revelation 5:5) to unlock it. Surely, this is a principle; the treasures have been unlocked. Treasures are just sitting there unlocked. We should encounter treasures like the poor lepers of 2 Kings 7:8-10 who discover that an enemy army had encamped and then fled Israel leaving all of its equipment. I have not unlocked anything. But like St. Peter's escape through a gate in Acts 12, I did not find this to be locked. Somehow, there must be a second speed, and it is not locked away from us. We can know this because Christ has prevailed to unlock it.

We have imaginations to summon, sufficient to pursue the second speed. Nothing stops us from imagining, even calculating it. And that is what theology is. Whether evilly directed, crazily directed, stupidly directed, randomly directed, or even well and wisely directed, theology is our imagining and reasoning about divine knowledge. We are doing the following thing exactly: "so that they should seek the Lord, in the hope that they might grope for Him and find Him, though He is not far from each one of us" — Acts 17:27 NKJV.

Notice that this passage contains groping for God and even mentions ubiquity. Let's call them the "groping group." We are in the groping group. We are doing that very thing. We are trying to find our way. Our groping is directed under the discipline described at the outset.

Our imagination, then, even as we continue to feel our way in the darkness, has full power to reason about this issue of speed. It is time to ask, "Would the second speed have to be miraculous, or can physics know it?"

We Have Found Our Loved Ones
Chapter VIII

It is interesting that our science of physics allows for a special case. If that special case applies, the second speed would not have to be magical. It could be merely physical. The special case, however, applies to just one and only one entity. This entity is something we are touching all the time, and we know a lot about it. This entity may move with no limit on its speed; it is space itself.

Space itself need not ever move, but it **can** move. And it can move at **any** speed; it is not limited to the speed of light. Space has that unlimited-movement property. And space cannot excel GOD, so GOD is the only entity with sufficient size and functional capability to do all that space does. Ease of movement applies to God and to space. We are inside of GOD, and we are inside of space.

How are these related? It seems blasphemous to say, "Space is GOD and GOD is space." It is better to say, "Space is an attribute of GOD." Space cannot be a mere creature of GOD because it would be, in size, His equal; but He has no equal.

Space has at least one of God's attributes. We could eventually come to the place where we would say, "Space is GOD." By this reasoning, space is either controlled by a will, or it **has** a will. That will can be none other than the will of GOD.

There is another way to think of space. The physical things in the universe are not God. If they were part of God, that would be some form of pantheism, but they are not. God created them, God could repudiate them, God could destroy them. To God, the universe could be trivial. But because He has given it importance, important it is. As for space, if God is holding it, it is not God, either.

Space is elastic; it bends and stretches. Physics teachers ask students to imagine an ant crawling along a rubber band. The ant's top speed is maybe one foot per second, but the ant will exceed its top speed if the rubber band is stretched forward as the ant crawls forward. This explains how, within the general theory of relativity, a speed faster than the speed of light is allowed. Another theory, the special theory of relativity, is for a local area; it has the speed of light as a hard speed limit. We, however, are interested in the entire universe. General relativity certainly applies to it; it has no hard speed limit. Later, when we look at Matthew 24:31, we will hear Jesus describe two regions. As I judge it, in one of those regions, "the four winds," the special theory of relativity applies, and in the other region, "from one end of heaven to the other," i.e., the entire universe, the general theory of relativity applies. The same pair of regions appears in Psalms 108:4, "Thy mercy is great above the heavens: and thy truth reacheth unto the clouds." We will obey those limits, as physics dictates. Admittedly, we have a fantastic speed to justify, but there are many other fantastic things in physics.

Like the rubber band which carries the ant along, so saints and angels are carried along. Like a rubber band, to move at the necessary second speed, space itself must move you as it moves itself and move itself as it moves you. The exclusive method would therefore mean that a person would have to be transported by GOD **personally**. Only you are you, only GOD is space, and neither can be delegated to another. The next section on John 1:51 will clarify this. Otherwise, we sentient beings, whether heavenly saint or angel or mortal saint on earth, would be stuck at the pokey old speed of light. To visualize this, please let me advance a fictional concept and quickly withdraw it. Children's fiction has produced the concept of a "magic carpet," but it pales in comparison to heavenly transport by heaven's King.

You may be wondering, "Could the Bible confirm any of this

stuff?" Well, of course, otherwise I would not trouble you with this theory.

Squeaketh the mouse, "I'm getting back in the prayer line. I need a magic carpet."

The verse of greatest importance is a frank statement. Jesus took credit—full credit—for this divine transport, "Verily, verily, I say unto you, Hereafter ye shall see heaven open, and the angels of God ascending and descending upon the Son of man." —John 1:51. This geometry, which is like a ladder, Jacob's ladder, of ubiquity, is confirmed in John 3:13, "And no man hath ascended up to heaven, but he that came down from heaven, even the Son of man which is in heaven." The ladder must reach that far, and it does. And, "I am the vine, ye are the branches: He that abideth in me, and I in him, the same bringeth forth much fruit: for **without me ye can do nothing**." —John 15:5 (emphasis added).

Conclusion: Individual power to ascend to God's heaven does not ever exist, even for angels. Jesus does it all. He transports us to heaven, and He transports saints and angels in heaven.

You certainly know the next one. Less direct but with great emphasis, there is that great spiritual statement, "I am the way, the truth, and the life: no man cometh unto the Father, but by me."—John 14:6. These great statements can now be applied in an additional way— geometrically. You understood them before; now you understand them even more. Although geometry is of trivial importance compared to thy soul, geometry helps you understand these statements as physical, real absolutes.

Returning to John 1:51, this passage reveals that angels cannot, of their own power, travel at sufficient speed to perform GOD's command to gather His guests. But with God's help, in this case Jesus' help, they travel with God at divine speed. Apparently, the angels are sent to be messengers, escorts, or entourage; but the transporter is God Himself. This theory finds God being a helpful host to angels and saints. **He performs that service to a previously unforeseen degree. He is indeed a host!** Let no one presume to think that one can do anything for God in heaven or on the earth. It is God who works.

Next, how fast must this form of travel be? Jesus said, "For as lightning that comes from the east is visible even in the west, so will be the coming of the Son of man."— Matthew 24:27. This expresses the suddenness of His coming in earth time.

Now, let us consider our own experiences. When you see lightning in the sky, that image travels to you at the speed of light taking a millisecond or more, depending on distance. If the "coming" or "gathering" is a journey of 93 billion light years, the result is still just as sudden in earth time. This proves that there is a second speed and reveals what it is. The speed of the coming of the Lord is, therefore, approximately 93 billion light years per millisecond. This would be 93 times 5,878,625,000,000 = 546,712,125,000,000 miles per millisecond, about 2.9 trillion times the speed of light. Yes, it could be faster than my number, so I don't really know it. But I know about this speed. I am bold to estimate it. It is just a number that God has chosen. I, and now you, have brazenly looked at GOD and lived, peering into that speed that He chooses as divine. I am ignoring the need to multiply this speed by the number of saints to get them all gathered within a millisecond, so 546,712,125,000,000 miles per millisecond is a minimum speed. I name it as "Jesus' minimum speed to gather the elect." There is no limit to how fast He can go; this is just the minimum.

There is no need to believe this. But assuming it's true, of what possible relevance is this knowledge?

Jesus tells us why divine speed is important to us. The key verse is Matthew 24:31, "And he shall send his angels with a great sound of a trumpet, and they shall gather together his elect from the four winds, from one end of heaven [ouranos] to the other." As we have shown, the divine speed is a necessity to accomplish this gathering. A heavenly gathering must happen promptly, or else

God's invitation is being ignored. Otherwise, He, the great king, would have to wait eons for his word to be fulfilled.

GOD, of course, **could** choose to wait, but He never **has** to. GOD need not wait even for a millisecond.

We Have Found Our Loved Ones
Chapter IX

To review, only by travel at this divine second speed can the elect be gathered quickly enough "from one end of heaven to the other." Suppose, as we have reasoned that the gathering speed is indeed 93 billion light years per millisecond. The gathering of the saints in heaven would only require a millisecond. When GOD is ready for something to happen, it happens. No other theory aids our understanding so well. We have comprehended not only the speed but also the rapidity of heavenly events—they happen "quickly." But let us consider next their importance on the Earth.

You probably have deduced from many scriptures that a reward is given at such gatherings. It is helpful to consider some examples. Revelation 22:12, "And, behold, I come quickly; and my reward is with me, to give every man according as his work shall be." Yes, the rewards are influenced by the merits of good works. But do not take that the wrong way. Revelation 14:13 explains, “their works do follow them.” It does not say their works propel them to heaven.

It is God who motivates and enables the action of good works. Analogous to His help with heavenly travel, God does it all. You now understand faith and works better than most preachers and theologians. I trust that they understand inspiration. But you understand works geometrically, whereas they generally do not.

Read Isaiah 40:10, "Behold, the Lord GOD will come with strong hand, and his arm shall rule for him: behold, his reward is with him, and his work before him.” We are His work, and we are before Him. This prophesied of Christ’s saving work, which He completed.

His reward includes everlasting pleasure, fellowship, friendship, and love. The love is His love as well as the love of those with Him. Thus, “the LORD my God shall come, and all the saints with thee.”—Zechariah 14:5.

Love is shared at the gatherings. Again, this love is by all, for all, and all means “all.” This happens to all the saints.

The air just above us is the closest place that fits the historical notion of heaven, and the gathering to greet each individual saint at their death happens right there, in the air. Consider, how can I know that there is a “gathering to greet each individual saint at their death”? There must have been prior gatherings because at the coming of the Lord, as we just read in Matthew 24:31, the saints are already elevated; none are gathered from under the ground. The geometrical limits of Matthew 24:31 do not allow that even one of God's elect has been waiting in the grave, after the Ascension, supposedly. Notice how Jesus presents the soon-to-be Ascension, "a time is coming and has now come when the dead shall hear the voice of the Son of God" —John 5:25. By ubiquity and His word, they would be hearing Him say this.

I reasoned, like most others, that before the Ascension, the Old Testament saints had to wait. But after the Ascension there is no waiting. This "change" seems confirmed by John 12:32, "And I, if I be lifted up from the earth, will draw all men unto me." This is also confirmed by Colossians 3:4, "When Christ, who is our life, shall appear, then shall ye also appear with him in glory." Again, "appear," sounds like a millisecond to gather them. Zechariah 9:14, "And the LORD shall be seen over them, and his arrow shall go forth as the lightning."

What about my error that the Old Testament saints had to wait in limbo? Yes, I had read that but not in the Bible. The Bible says, "And Enoch walked with God: and he was not; for God took him." —Genesis 5:24. This was a blessed event as confirmed by Hebrews 11:5. No waiting was implied; Enoch was translated. "Elijah went up by a whirlwind into heaven." —2 Kings 2:11. Nobody told him to wait. There is a teaching that the "Bosom of Abraham," mentioned by Jesus, was a place of comfort in the earth where the Old Testament saints had to wait. That seems to be supported by the vision seen by the Witch of Endor in 1 Samuel 28. What a ridiculous source. She asked King Saul, "Whom shall I bring up unto thee?" She was already assuming hell or hades as a holding place. Taking the words of the Witch of Endor as a wrong way indicator, we need to look up instead. But have we not just quoted Jesus confirming "waiting"?

Let's look again. Remember that omnipresence is supreme exclusivity. Thus, we can more perfectly understand Jesus, "And no man hath ascended up to heaven, but he that came down from heaven, even the Son of man which is in heaven (John 3:13)." This is a fundamental claim of exclusivity. We habitually use the deceptive figure of speech, "gone to heaven," implying that created beings have power to go to heaven. Better to express it as in the account of Enoch, "was taken." This provides a simpler theory because it is not necessary to "wait" or determine "where" the waiting occurs. There is no limbo; this is a simpler theory. Ubiquity has enabled us to victoriously solve this issue, trampling over hordes of theologians.

Squeaketh the mouse, “Alas, poor Theologian. I knew him well.”

What about, “a time is coming and has now come when the dead will hear the voice of the Son of God”? The gatherings are to the Lord. With Jesus in heaven, the gatherings belong there. With Jesus on earth, the gatherings belong here. It may be hard to accept but consider this. With Jesus descended to hades, a gathering could have happened there. Remember this, “… the graves were opened; and many bodies of the saints which slept arose, and came out of the graves after his resurrection, and went into the holy city, and appeared unto many.” —Matt. 27:53. This happened at the time of Jesus’ resurrection. The key word is “many,” which is not “all.” The next gathering after his resurrection includes, of course, saints whose bodies had been buried nearby to Jerusalem, locus of the gathering.

The soul makes the body alive. As usual each of their souls was transported personally by Jesus to the gathering. While stopping at their own graves, it would be impossible for their bodies not to be resurrected at the presence of the Lord, along with their souls. This strange event has now been solved by ubiquity.

Let us return to thoughts of heaven. How can we confirm that the locations of gatherings of the saints include those “in the air”?

First Thessalonians 4:17 says, "Then we which are alive and remain shall be caught up together with them in the clouds, to meet the Lord in the air: and so shall we ever be with the Lord."

There are several mysteries here. In spite of the massive size of the universe with its myriad of interesting, beautiful, and glorious gathering places, the location of the gatherings is in a rather humble, homely, homespun place, namely the air of planet Earth—even more specifically, "in the clouds." Clouds do sometimes touch the mountains, can mountains qualify? The Mount of Transfiguration was complete with a touch by a cloud (Matthew 17:5). This was a visible gathering for our edification. The number of humans from heaven was plural (Moses, Elijah, and Jesus), signifying all the saints. The number of humans from earth was plural (Peter, James, John, and Jesus), signifying us as mortals. Christ was with the mortals matching the divine fourth man of Daniel 3:25 and His oath of John 15:15. Christ is included with those from heaven, because He is from heaven. This is instructive, but in general the gatherings are invisible to us, while we are still mortal. (An exception might be at the point of death, Acts 7:56.) Take special note that there was no contact between the saints and the mortals —except via the Christ who is friend and Lord to both.

While our gaze is at the mountain tops, consider Psalm 121:1-

2 in the Catholic Bible (where the numbering is 120:1-2), "I have lifted up my eyes to the mountains, from whence help shall come to me. My help is from the Lord, who made heaven and earth." Combining (1) our theory, (2) that clouds sometimes touch the mountains, and (3) the need for help, we find yet another literal statement of truth hidden in poetry. This psalm, a great favorite, fits well. This is especially the case when we consider that judgments are given at the gatherings. The divine judgments deliver the saints on Earth from destruction, such as Daniel 7:9-10, Revelation 4, etc. These are, indeed, wonderful gifts, too. You do not have to die or fly to benefit from the judgments rendered at a gathering.

Now, note "clouds" may also refer to clouds of stars. There are so many stars in the night sky that there seem to be clouds among the stars, because they are so many and so far away. Those clouds are, or could signify, the saints in their far away positions. And they come with the Lord. "Behold, one like the Son of man came with the clouds of heaven." —Daniel 7:13. And, "Behold, he cometh with clouds." —Revelation 1:7.

The saints also have near positions. Near, they are hidden in God and invisible to us. Whether near or far, they are clouds of witnesses as St. Paul teaches, "We also are compassed about with so great a cloud of witnesses."—Hebrews 12:1. Near or far, "from the four winds, from one end of heaven to the other," the saints are above and among clouds. Clouds anywhere should remind us of them. The saints are not limited to merely two places, of course. The span of their dwellings and travels is the entire universe and more. Whether they, the saints, and our friends, are in the air or among the stars, you can visualize all by use of your imagination, just as God urged Abraham to do in Genesis 15:5.

Having toured the heavens, let us look at the Mount of Transfiguration experience through our lens. On the mount there were three perfect ones, the Lord and two of his saints. There were three fallible persons, Peter, James, and John. The three perfect ones, of course, made no errors. We can guess what will happen next.

> Peter said to Jesus, 'Lord, it is good for us to be here. If you wish, I will put up three shelters–one for You, one for Moses, and one for Elijah.' While he was still speaking, a bright cloud enveloped them, and a voice from the cloud said, 'This is My Son, whom I love; with Him I am well pleased. Listen to Him!' When the disciples heard this, they fell face down to the ground, terrified. – Matthew 17:4-6

The mortals were silent as they received the testimony of none other than God the Father.

Many have tried to determine why Moses and Elijah were chosen for this honor—to represent the saints. Most theories have merit. They were notable and exemplary as mortals on the earth, but we know of some of their errors. And their exits from the earth went heavenward, Moses to a mountain top and Elijah into heaven itself. As a testimony to faith, Moses' critical mistake was, "Because ye believed me not" —Numbers 20:12. So Moses, who represents the law, was trumped by faith or for the lack of it. He was, nevertheless, given honors that were not given to any other man, most especially this honor,

> **Moses climbed Mount Nebo from the plains of Moab to the top of Pisgah, across from Jericho. There the Lord showed him the whole [promised] land. And Moses the servant of the Lord died there in Moab, as the Lord had said.**

The Lord God, in a Christophany as I take it, "buried him in Moab, in the valley opposite Beth Peor, but to this day no one knows where his grave is." —Deuteronomy 34:1-5. (Jude 9 testifies to the importance of keeping Moses' grave a secret.) Moses received this unique honor, but Elijah needed no burial as was witnessed by 50 of the sons of the prophets, "Behold, there appeared a chariot of fire, and horses of fire, and parted them both asunder; and Elijah went up by a whirlwind into heaven." —2 Kings 2:11. Elijah was thus honored, despite fleeing Jezebel's chariots. Moses and Elijah are perfect examples for the increase of our knowledge.

Although they were wonderful men, Moses was just a man and Elijah was just a man (James 5:17).

Squeaketh the mouse, "I am getting back in the prayer line, I need a chariot."

So, we can be confident that the saints gather above us. But our knowledge is weak, "For now we see through a glass, darkly; but then face to face: now I know in part; but then shall I know even as also I am known." —1 Corinthians 13:12.

We Have Found Our Loved Ones
Chapter X

We have mentioned angels only when scripture does, but they are present whether mentioned or not. A person, even though one believes in angels, might never think of them, and take them completely for granted. It is good to say a liturgical phrase you may have heard, “With Angels and Archangels and All the Company of Heaven.” If you thought it was poetry, clever rhetoric, or just holy talk, you missed that it is really the simplest statement of literal, geometric truth. It describes an earthly ceremony along with a heavenly gathering. This event happens many times per second because there are numerous receptions per minute of new saints at their deaths. But death is not the only occasion for gatherings. A church service, no matter how small, includes divine company (Matthew 18:20, Hebrews 12:22). The saints surround us above like the material clouds we see, momentarily. And, momentarily, they are gone to their various pleasures.

A question arises, “Why would the heavenly congregation not stay for an entire one-hour church service?”

Answer: That would be 3,600,000 milliseconds. That would be like we mortals staying through a 3,600,000-hour church service, more than 40 years.

Squeaketh the mouse, “This seat is getting really hard.”

I see no function that requires a saint or all the saints to see us as individuals on the Earth. Earthly information would rarely be perfect, that is, up to their standard. They have a nearly continuous flow of new saints and even martyrs to provide perfect information about the Earth. They have excellent firsthand insight about what is important to the church on Earth, without directly viewing us.

In favor of their viewing us, as well as deriding the Lord’s enemies, are promises to view vindications, “He that dwelleth in heaven shall laugh at them: and the Lord shall deride them.” —Psalm 2:4 Catholic Bible. And, “His heart is established, he shall not be afraid, until he see his desire upon his enemies.” —Psalm 112:8.

Another issue is their quickness or our slowness. If they did view us, it would be a still image, not a movie. I call this “quick Heaven, slow Earth.”

And now for the next objection. I seek not to destroy mysticism, although I know my reasoning seems mechanical. I am willing to give mysticism its due unless it contradicts scripture.

Now do this. Focus on the personal. Here is why this leads you to mysticism. We have shown through the example of the Eucharist that God's ubiquity is personal, so much so that it is shocking. You, me, all creatures, the stars, and so forth—everything that there is—is touching GOD, all the time. We are inside of God in everything we do. Every sin we ever committed happened inside of God. This, then, justifies the judgment. This certainly calls for mysticism, or, better yet, absolution.

Faith in the omnipresence of God is a spiritual abundance. Such a faith is richer than one without awareness of God's abiding presence. This is not about avoiding a condemnation. True, avoiding the condemnation of Ben-hadad (explained above) is certainly to be desired. In the age of grace, maybe that does not apply, anyway. The Christian revelation has the characteristic that closing the door to hell becomes a triviality compared to the glory that is instantly within. "If you only knew what God gives."—John 4:10, Good News Translation. In addition to that, because you now believe in omnipresence, you have a splendor that you did not have before.

I know you can scarcely believe this. Lucifer, of course, knew that he was splendid, and fell. He really was splendid, but it did not immunize him from a fall. You, unlike Lucifer, by the knowledge of ubiquity, know that God's presence is your help and your only righteous power. Although you have no spiritual beauty except what descends to you from God, that gift proceeds from Him and is more glory than you can handle.

True to ubiquity, glory bubbles up within, according to John 4:14,

> **But whosoever drinketh of the water that I shall give him shall never thirst; but the water that I shall give him shall be in him a well of water springing up into everlasting life.**

You are unable to help yourself without it, just as you are unable to fly unaided to the far side of the universe. But with God all things are possible.

It might help to relate all things, including heaven, to our own earthly experiences of visiting others. During our earthly existence, we physically visit others, sometimes to render help. Other times, we need help. But usually visits have nothing to do with help but are for enjoyment or perhaps obligation. Need and obligation do not apply in heaven, so let us be careful to leave them out as motives. Heaven is free will and thy will shall be perfect; there is no obligation.

So, what about visiting; is there visiting? Notice the range of locations mentioned in this fragment from Deut. 4:32, "… ask now of the days that are past… since the day that God created man upon the earth and ask from the one side of heaven unto the other." These cannot be empty words; these words must tell. In this sermon, Moses rhetorically dares the hearers to ask ancestors on Earth and in Heaven if any people have ever been granted the special relationship that Israel was granted by God. You and I could spout fictional hyperboles, but the Holy Spirit inspiring Moses only used true possibilities.

There are passages that fortify Matthew 24:31, where we also find the elect elevated after death. In Deut. 4:32 the hearers are the elect and will indeed go "from the one side of heaven unto the other." Here is what "ask from the one side of heaven unto the other" means. A saint (you) can count on God's help to visit and ask and interview all the saints since Adam. The manner of that you now comprehend. Travel to their mansions would be at that second—divine speed, by means of the Lord helping you.

The whole universe is a dwelling. God "stretcheth out the heavens as a curtain, and spreadeth them out as a tent to dwell in"— Isaiah 40:22.

Traversing the entire universe will be quick and effortless with the Lord's help, and you will have it. John 14:2, "In my Father's house are many mansions: if it were not so, I would have told you.

I go to prepare a place for you." There are more than a trillion galaxies. Galaxies are, as I take it, these mansions. Thy dwelling, yes, your dwelling, your galaxy, will be vast, beautiful, and awesome. The distance between dwellings would be many light years. But at the second speed, dwelling in God's heaven is enabled —by God, personally. Dwelling in and traveling about heaven is therefore instantaneous, effortless, easy, satisfying, beautiful, rich, blissful, varied, restful, exciting, opulent, luxurious, joyful, dynamic, bejeweled, crowned, and royal, to name a few descriptors. The saints cast down their crowns, fall down, and worship the Lamb. In other words, their bliss and their worship exceed our understanding and contain myriads of immeasurable aspects of glory. The heavenly saints rest in their own individual galaxies (as beds) and rouse themselves to go worship the Lord. They dwell in the universe like it is a city because it is a city, the city of the saints.

And it is a city of singing, "Let the saints be joyful in glory: let them sing aloud upon their beds." —Psalm 149:5.

We Have Found Our Loved Ones
Chapter XI

We have been successfully reasoning about divine subjects as physical phenomena, not "as if" they are physical phenomena, but rather "as" the physical phenomena they actually are. True, on the subject of God, we can only know what God reveals. Using not two forms of logic but just one, we are able to reason our way using revealed knowledge plus our scientific observations. I do not say that reason takes us to God. No, we now comprehend that, geometrically, God takes us to God. This methodology appears to easily allow us to solve spiritual mysteries. Indeed, I think so.

Squeaketh the mouse, "Hey, I just woke up. Is it over?"

We Have Found Our Loved Ones
Chapter XII

Because we comprehend there is a nearness of the saints sometimes, one spiritual issue cannot be avoided.

A significant percentage of more than a billion Roman Catholics rely heavily on intercession by the saints in heaven. Many excellent Roman Catholic churchmen and laypersons do it, and what they do is none of my business. But here is the issue. What you have just read could dramatically increase prayers to the saints, or even induce others to do it. Therefore, I must unravel this issue. I must take seriously those supposed communications between mortals and immortals.

I do not mean to belittle the most heartfelt mourning for the dead. Most anything might happen there without condemnation. I confine my comments to prayers to saints long dead that none of us knew.

Specifically, let me prove, if I can, the Protestant view which constrains us strongly not to pray to the saints. The Augsburg Confession in a section titled, "The Cult of Saints," states, "Scriptures do not teach us to pray to the saints or seek their help, for the only mediator, propitiator, high priest, and intercessor whom the Scriptures set before us is Christ." How hard is this prohibition? And does Deuteronomy 18:10-11 apply?

> There shall not be found among you any one that maketh his son or his daughter to pass through the fire, or that useth divination, or an observer of times, or an enchanter, or a witch, or a charmer, or a consulter with familiar spirits, or a wizard, or a necromancer.

It has the most direct prohibition of necromancy, a word also translated as "that seeketh the truth from the dead." – Catholic Bible. It is included on a list along with some hideous things.

(((Tappert, T. G. (2000, c1959). The Augsburg Confession: Translated from the Latin (The Confession of Faith: I, art. xxi, par. 2). Philadelphia: Fortress Press.)))

Squeaketh the mouse, "Wow. Did I sleep all the way to Halloween?"

Why is there an emphatic prohibition, anyway? Simple answer: they are perfect, and we are not. Here is what I surmise from Bible examples, "The saints are perfected, and this is what makes communication destined to go wrong." Examples provide a cautionary tale, not a prohibition. (Another simple answer will be available when we treat the physics of such communications.) An example is,

> **I fell at his feet to worship him. But he said to me, 'See that you do not do that! I am your fellow servant, and of your brethren who have the testimony of Jesus. Worship God!' – Rev. 19:10**

Note that prayer and worship are inseparable. That is what happened when a pretty good mortal, St. John, meets someone who is perfect. It does not go well. Our depraved sinfulness that adheres to us and their perfection do not mix. And I think it is a fair interpretation that they are also so impressive that we, who are not accustomed to glory, would have a strong urge to worship them. Even though they love us, and we love them, we do not mix yet. Eventually, we will communicate in fellowship forever. That does not begin until after we also are perfected.

As in Rev. 19:10, until the day we are perfected, a saint will only, most likely, be able to rebuke us. We must await our graduation to their state, and it is good we are not anxious to go. We have business here. Faith gives us the confidence and the patience to abide. Let us be mannerly toward the saints and not try to specifically communicate.

Some day we will all meet Saint Mary, the mother of Jesus. Even Luther liked and used the term, "Mother of God." Because

Christ is undivided, we are well justified to use and like this term. The Reformation was not about Mary. I do, however, take the position that in spite of this true title, not even one person on earth has ever met her after her death and before theirs. It is reasonable to demand proof of this statement.

It has long been noticed about the Gospel of Luke, that there are accounts of the life of Mary that must have come either from Mary herself or from someone very close to her. Which is it? Here is the passage that proves to me that Luke's sources include Mary herself. It could be called, "Jesus' family statement."

> **And it was told him by certain which said, 'Thy mother and thy brethren stand without, desiring to see thee.' And he [Jesus] answered and said unto them, 'My mother and my brethren are these which hear the word of God, and do it.' – Luke 8:20-21**

Some might say, therefore, that Mary did not talk to Luke. But I see something. The first time I heard this passage, I was surprised, make that flummoxed. When this happened to Mary, I think she was, too. It took years for me to understand. It may have taken years for her to understand. As I see it, the Holy Spirit would call forth the most deeply affected witness.

By the time Mary told this to Luke, she wanted the entire Church to know this. That witness was her duty, and it was a good and holy work for her to report this. Mary wanted the Church to know this critically important pronouncement. Faith is trust and agreement with God. Mary knew that it was the very best thing for Jesus to convey. It's simple; it's stark. Jesus declared his rank-and-file followers to be Mary's equal. It is amazing also that it does not require the entirety of the Church to constitute her equal; no, any member in good standing is individually her equal. Never mind that every Christian, including Martin Luther, would insist, "No. I cannot be her equal!" But it is not up to us; Christ specified it. Nor can it be countermanded by any church official, any church council, or even the whole Church of Jesus Christ.

There is a theory, make that a winsome and beloved doctrine, that Mary continues to have present day missions. She has a special intercessory mission, giving frequent directions to the Church, telling the world how to achieve world peace, etc. It would be more scripturally proper to plug in the name of any living Christian because it is we, our angels, and the Holy Ghost who have all missions in this world below.

I find it depressing to suppose that the glorious, blissful heavenly sojourn of St. Mary or any other individual saint is perturbed so frequently. (I'll calculate how many later.) All the saints in unison could be perturbed as in Rev. 6:10, perhaps at proper intervals, to be studied later. According to Rev. 14:13, individually the saints are not perturbed at all, “Yea, saith the Spirit, that they may rest from their labors; and their works do follow them.” The works that the saints did on earth follow them to heaven; they are not working now.

Much is made of how Mary got to heaven. The Latin, *assumptio*, means "taking up." This word is true and scriptural as applied to the soul of any saint. Enoch was translated, and Elijah entered “into heaven” without dying. Jesus did die before ascending. Virtually all others are taken up after dying. Saint Paul sets all this straight,

> **Listen very carefully, I tell you a mystery [a secret truth decreed by God and previously hidden, but now revealed]; we will not all sleep [in death], but we will all be [completely] changed [wondrously transformed]. —1 Corinthians 15:51**
>
> ***comments are part of the Amplified Bible***

Observe that St. Paul told us there would be variations. The most important parts are, “we will all be” and “changed.” Differences do not matter; the result is what matters.

Mary’s *assumptio*, the Assumption of Mary, is celebrated on August 15 (since 1950). All of the Elect have those —*assumptios*. Your own *assumptio* will happen at your death.

Now, consider the dogma that Mary was taken up body and

soul into heaven. I am not saying no to that; it was done before. Elijah did it. As I judge it, feel free to believe in the Assumption of Mary, and even believe that her *assumptio* delivered her body and soul to heaven. Canonical scriptures do not support this, but it cannot be disproven.

I like the Immaculate Conception of Mary, celebrated December 8 (Roman Rite), December 9 (Byzantine Rite), August 13 (Alexandrian Rite) according to Wikipedia. But this would mean that the incarnation of Christ was a two-step process, a special conception for Mary then one for Jesus. This is not the simplest theory, so Occam's Razor points away from it. Direct actions by God, such as, "And God said, Let there be light: and there was light," require only one step. The Catholic Bible is even better, "And God said: Be light made. And light was made." If the Bible had said, "There is light," that would be zero steps, like "This is my body" is a present fact. We have studied this and can now confirm that the Eucharist has zero steps.

I like the Immaculate Conception but cannot believe it.

The real issue is the notion that the Immaculate Conception of Mary and her supposedly special *assumptio* reveals and justifies a vast, ongoing ministry of visitations. Jesus, of course, failed to mention these many advantages to visits by his mother. But He did tell us that we would be greatly advantaged by the coming of the Holy Spirit.

I am sorry to have to say this, but visions of Mary are not Mary herself communicating with us. They are communications, but not from her. No dream or vision about Mother Mary coming to you is a communication from Mary herself. No dream or vision about your loved ones coming to you is a communication from your loved ones themselves. That is what they are not, but what are they?

Consider a passage from Luke, KJV, “the virgin's name was Mary. And the angel came in unto her, and said…” or from the Catholic Bible, “and the virgin's name was Mary. And the angel being come in, said unto her.” Notice that the angel had to be very close to be able to communicate. Very close, perhaps even touching her ear. This reveals much. Why do so many people think they are more powerful than an angel as regards communication? And what shall we say about those visions and dreams of Mary? She is far away. We are well able to treat the physics of this.

Simple question: Are there examples in the Bible of created beings, that is, angels or humans, communicating with one another at a great distance?

Simple answer: No.

Remember: By ubiquity, communication with God is at zero distance. Referring to Daniel 10:12-13, an angel required 21 days to bring a message from the throne of God, but Daniel had communicated with God instantly. That passage is recounted in the Bible so that we will know the truth and not be misled.

People experience visions, dreams, and voices. These are communications from the angels who are touching us or from the Lord directly. The important question is not of physics but of righteousness or wickedness. Are the angels causing such a vision, dream, or voice, either evil or righteous? There are both kinds, as you are aware. It is very difficult for anyone to know which type of spirit is involved, even for persons of great discernment. If it is an emanation of evil, the consequences of following such a vision may be dire. First Kings 22:20-22 provides a vivid example for our edification on how easy it is to be deceived. Great skepticism is called for. A hasty evaluation is not adequate, we may need to take a few years. And next, a presumptive falsehood must be tackled. It is fear that captures and harms many persons.

Not all these experiences are benign. Very many persons have had terrifying dreams, visions, or voices all seemingly from the dead. If vivid, this kind of occurrence can be horrific. First, observe that your mind retains a memory of the voice, appearance, and attitudes of loved ones departed. It remains there, stored in your brain. By merely touching the location of that memory, a wicked spirit could give you quite a vivid experience. Such an impression does not constitute a true communication with the dead. It should most likely be regarded as just a devil's trick. However, to help you, your guardian angel could communicate to you in much the same way, so "test the spirits." —1 John 4:1.

I say, "Beware." I say, "Be wise." In 2 Kings 17:16, "They bowed down to all the starry host." Does this passage describe pagans only? No, it describes God's people. It was one of the blasphemies that, along with the matter of Ben-hadad, led to the permanent exile of the Lost Tribes. It did not help them that "all the starry host" would include holy angels and saints. This prohibition is confirmed by Rev. 19:10 and 22:9. The object of St. John's errant worship in Rev. 19:10 was not identified as an angel, but in Rev. 22:9 that being was identified as an angel. The principle was the same, however.

Consider a judgment pronounced on the southern kingdom in Zephaniah 1:4-5,

> I will stretch out my hand against Judah
> and against all who live in Jerusalem.
> I will destroy every remnant of Baal worship in this place,
> the very names of the idolatrous priests—

those who bow down on the roofs
to worship the starry host,
those who bow down and swear by the LORD
and who also swear by Molek.

There are two religions operating at the same time. The other religious practice is stepping all over the true religion of the Jews. Worship of the "starry host" was anathema to Judaism. Under Old Testament Law false religion was punished. St. Stephen placed this as one of the causes of the exile of the southern kingdom, Judah, "God turned, and gave them up to serve the host of heaven" —Acts 7:42. In the age of grace, we may hope that these punishments are omitted or softened, but it is still wrong to worship the angels and saints. The saints and holy angels are our friends, equals, and family. Just as it is wrong to worship our friends on earth, it is wrong to worship them from earth toward heaven after they die. So, where do we draw the line?

We Have Found Our Loved Ones

Chapter XIII

At the statue of a saint is a perfectly fine place to offer a prayer to God. If you choose to kneel, that is fine also. But what about a case that appears similar? Someone will say, "I bowed down and prayed before the statue of a saint (pick one). That was because I wanted the saint, like our friend St. Mary, to intercede for me."

Squeaketh the mouse, "No way there are patron saints of cats."

(((https://www.catholic.org/saints/patron.php lists 1,776 patron saints including one for cats.)))

Squeaketh the mouse, "It's not a nice thing to call poor St. Gertrude of Nivelles the patron saint of cats. That is the same as calling her the devil."

This presents a few issues. The one thing I choose to shout from the mountain tops is "Ubiquity." Your distance to God and the distances of heavenly saints to God are exactly the same. The distance is zero in all cases. Think about it. No person, place, or thing is physically closer to God than any other. But our distance to a heavenly saint is not zero; it is a great distance. Avoiding prayer to God yourself but praying to a distant third party instead, may not be pleasing to either.

To prove distance is important and prevents communication, ponder this,

> **After this I looked, and, behold, a door was opened in heaven: and the first voice which I heard was as it were of a trumpet [this is strange, it is certainly not a human] talking with me; which said, Come up hither, and I will shew thee things which must be hereafter. – Revelation 4:1**

A trumpet sound is also found in the key verse of this study, Matt. 24:31.

It is a wonderful privilege for me to prove Charles Haddon Spurgeon wrong. Life is good. In a sermon entitled, "A Door Opened in Heaven," he viewed Rev. 4:1 as a "door of intercourse," "door of observation," and "to each of us there will be a door of entrance opened, by which we shall enter in through the golden gate into the city." According to Spurgeon, John did not have to go to heaven to communicate or see. God has the power to do it Spurgeon's way, but that would make God into a mechanism, apparatus, or message center. It is important to note that the interpretation of the father of fundamentalism (which developed after him) did not produce a fundamentalist interpretation of Rev. 4:1. I have.

(((https://www.spurgeon.org/resource-library/sermons/a-door-opened-in-heaven/#flipbook/)))

For St. John to communicate with heavenly beings, he had to go where they were. Rev. 4:1 is in the Bible so that even a child could correct some Roman Catholic theologians. The ones who do need correction, flunking geometry, teach that an intercessory prayer to one of heaven's saints or angels can be made from earth to heaven. No, John had to go there before he could communicate. The invitation that came down to him was specifically not from a created being. It was from a trumpet.

Elsewhere in the Bible there are examples of communications from earthly mortals to saints, but these are not pleasant. We have already discussed the Witch of Endor in 1 Samuel 28:7-25. That passage ends with a prophecy of failure and death. Luke 16:19-31 is a desperate cry from hell. These were not sweet hours of prayer. These passages should not be treated fondly.

Next, we find John in heaven talking with a glorious being, who was probably an average citizen. John was sure his final salute should be to worship that being. Here is how it went. In both Rev. 19:10 and 22:9 we hear, "See that you do not do that." The inhabitants of God's heaven are first perfected. That includes their manners—they have perfect manners. Why don't the saints and angels worship each other or accept worship from us? Because that would be ill mannered, otherwise they would—such is the love and respect. John, a mere mortal, needs lots of instruction, and receives it.

We have found our loved ones, and we know how to behave with this knowledge. We know we do not have them now but will a little later. Instead of the saints to call upon, we and all creatures have our Creator God to call upon.

What if a saint seems to answer you or talk to you, say, from a statue? Such an experience is important for you to comprehend. Know that it is a deception. The person who has such an experience has a familiar spirit touching them. It is not communication from a dead person to a living person. You could use the terms "devils," "demons," "evil spirits," or "evil angels." These are the sources of such false communications. It is not your fault if you experience this, but it is your fault if you teach it to others.

We Have Found Our Loved Ones
Chapter XIV

Criticism is not a punishment per se. There is no Bible evidence that God has ever punished a pagan for praying to a pagan god. He has certainly criticized God's people for praying to pagan gods because they knew better. Various actions of pagans were hated, but simple prayer was not mentioned. We can suppose, without being able to prove it, that simple pagan prayer falls within a "safe harbor." I am still not saying I am proving this, but it makes sense that any simple prayer falls within a safe harbor. And it applies to all. It applies not only to pagans but especially to God-fearing believers.

We all desperately need this safe harbor, no matter how good we think our doctrines to be. We are all full of errors. And it should be acknowledged that we are all pagans compared to the holiness of God. Probably the ultimate proof of safe harbor happened in the aftermath of a murder. When Cain said to God that his punishment was too much for him (Genesis 4:13), we are amazed to read that he (the murderer) received a benefit.

We can now apply this to prayers to the saints. These prayers fall within the safe harbor. Therefore, there is no punishment for the simple act of prayer to a saint, if done in ignorance. But teaching that practice could be outside the safe harbor.

Clearly, God has not severely punished those who pray to saints among Roman Catholics. Perhaps He has not punished them at all. Is this dispensation, as I call it, permanent? And does this dispensation apply to the Roman Catholic teachers, priests, bishops, and the Pope? After all, James 3:1 applies to them, and me. The NIV has it as, "We who teach will be judged more strictly." I know not.

For hundreds of years, paganism and Christianity were side by side in the Roman Empire and elsewhere. There were a few crossovers of practices. Some take that as a source of veneration of the saints, but I see another origin. Praying to saints was not part of the primitive church for almost three centuries. It is important to note that that period included the "Gnostic challenge," which happened from about AD 100 to AD 250. It was a wide-ranging attack in every sense: intellectual, spiritual, sensual, and charismatic. There was a severe struggle to hold on to authenticity and sanity, and yes, I mean sanity, in the Church. Supposed prophets and apostles arose in local areas, opposed bishops, brought in many ideas from Hellenistic mystery religions, expressed esoteric knowledge that made out the gospel to be a bore, and drew to themselves many people. Libertine or legalistic ideas, as well as both together, swamped normal Christian thought.

Exasperated Christians wanted normal Christianity. That desire was expressed in a new word that caught on. Two Greek words, Katho and Likos, became katholikos and eventually (translating Greek to Latin and then to English) "catholic." We have additional meanings now, but originally it meant, "from the whole," that is "general, standard, and from the entirety of the church."

The word "universal," is sometimes used as a description of this original meaning of "Catholic." Universal is overly broad, however, unless it has "a fence around it." Every proper meaning of Catholic does have a fence around it. The fence was intended to be at the edge of standard Christianity. Whatever is universal inside standard Christianity has the meaning of universal to focus on. When Protestant churches recite the Apostles Creed, that is what they mean by, "I believe in the Holy Catholic Church." However, note others recite the very same creed but mean something different. Under that original meaning of "catholic," Christianity was saved by a catholic consensus.

Before the Gnostic challenge, there is no definite evidence of prayer to the saints. Remember, I am speaking only of the exact practice of a mortal on earth trying to pray to a saint in heaven and this being thought acceptable by church authorities.

After the horrendous experience of going through the Gnostic challenge, the Catholic Church appears in history. It now has a little bit of praying to the saints. This was and is a small matter compared to Gnosticism. It's like a soldier coming home victoriously from a war with a small scar. Is praying to the saints a scar? Is it small? I shall prove both.

So, praying to the saints was inside the moat by AD 300. Unfortunately, it became rampant in the pre-Reformation church. Praying to saints did not survive in Protestantism because one glance killed it. Did that influence Roman Catholicism? A little. That is where we are.

Is it my job to dissuade Roman Catholics from praying to saints? It is not, not in and of itself. My mission is to teach omnipresence. Fortunately, omnipresence or ubiquity is not hard to learn. You have learned it easily, whether or not you believe it. Ubiquity reveals that the distance from each and every created being to God is zero. Our distances to God and the distances of heavenly saints to God are the same—exactly zero. Both we and they are touching God.

As discussed, our distance to a heavenly saint is not zero; rather, it is a great distance. Let's call this the "Distance Issue," and number it "Stupidity No. 1" about God. The premise justifying prayers to saints is that God is more distant than the saints. They really say or imply that God is too busy, "Stupidity No. 2" about God. Worst of all, they teach that Jesus is a stern judge, "Stupidity No. 3" about God. This is a mess.

What, if anything, do we say? We need not spend time trying to change the thinking of a billion people. Only where you are urged to pray to saint so-and-so for the patronage of that saint, would you explain why not. Avoiding the issue is fine. After all, Christians are always at a great feast. We do not want to be ill mannered, even if others are. And that is the point; failing to have the attitude toward God evidenced by the saints themselves is out of place. In Revelation 4:10,11, the message from the saints is to worship our creator. Therefore, they found praying to the saints to be ill mannered in Revelation 19:10 and 22:9.

Are there any consequences for praying to the saints? In the age of grace, "I will love them freely," applies (Hosea 14:4). I conclude that there are no consequences for those who pray to the saints. Why then would I even discuss this subject? I mention it to discharge my duty and protect my soul from the taint of in any way encouraging worship or prayer toward the saints.

But I am not done.

Sad to ponder what happens to the trillion prayers addressed to Mary. Would God allow a saint in paradise to be tormented with such messages? I say not. To support this view, let us sift through Bible examples.

And what about the ways to communicate to a saint in heaven? How many communication paths are possible, given that we are not just fantasizing but are constrained to follow Bible examples and principles? Recall the long-distance communications in 1 Samuel 28:7-25 (supposedly downward communication anyway) and Luke 16:19-31 (the rich man was dead) were not pleasant or efficacious for the communicators. There is nothing to desire in these examples. In a major tell, St. John, in Revelation 4:1, was caught up all the way to heaven in order to communicate with heavenly beings in a normal way such as, "one of the elders said to me" (Revelation 5:5). His trip was efficacious for us all. Bear in mind the surprising rebuffs of St. John in Revelation 19:10 and 22:9 are tells. And, in a normal way, an angel talks with him in Revelation 10:9; they are face to face; this implies a short path.

On Earth we use technology to extend what a face-to-face meeting can accomplish. We might call it magic, but we don't mean that. We of the Earth use technology to communicate at the speed of light; but remember, the speed of light is a failure. To communicate to the far side of the universe, where Mary spends part of her time, something like 2.9 trillion times the speed of light is required, or she shall have gone to where her next blissful activity occurs before the message arrives. This is a way of saying that the distance issue applies.

You may be wondering, "Couldn't God be a communication enabler?" Yes, but God is not a mechanism or apparatus. He is not a message center. Everything that God does is controlled by His perfect will. He revealed his will to the Israelites, causing them to know that He is truly a person. He revealed his inner thoughts as, "I, the LORD your God, am a jealous God"—Exodus 20:5. It does not seem consistent with that for us to suppose He would to be completely pleased with his children praying to another.

The physics does not work either. A prayer would have to travel to one of the "ends of heaven." A saint would, now and then, be located at that extremity. For it to reach them with only our feeble human agency is to call upon magic. The philosophy that I am teaching disallows magic and does not ever need it.

I said I would prove that no cleric, preacher, priest, bishop, pope, some charismatic-Protestant "prophet," medium, or witch knows the disposition of your loved one in the hereafter. Here is what we know about the movement of such knowledge. The distance issue applies for a downward distance, even though the distance is far less than across the universe. God is not a mechanism, so He would have to have a desire that such knowledge be provided. There is one valid example of this. For a teaching purpose, Jesus did it in Luke 16:19-31. Rarity and the eminence of the person who revealed that information implies that this kind of knowledge is privileged only to God. This an exception that proves the rule.

Consider this: If God has mercy on some dead rascal, and if we were to know it, that would lower the bar of acceptable human behavior—maybe by a lot. We may think, "Old so-and-so made it. I can do anything I want!" Such a knowledge will not direct us toward righteousness. In First Samuel 28:7-25, the Witch of Endor claimed to call up spirits; but again, she is not to be our guide. Both Purgatory and any knowledge of its supposed inhabitants should not be considered valid.

A question might arise about angels having and transferring knowledge of the dead. An evil angel would do that for an evil purpose, most likely with falsehoods. A holy angel would seek to obey the will of God, and therefore, speak only what is in your best interest. So, the holy transfer of knowledge either does not happen or is natural. Perhaps after many years, an answer could be divined by anyone. The theory I have in mind is that blessings somehow follow the saints and their posterity as Psalm 112 testifies. It would still be a guess, but it would not require a priest.

We, among the other God-fearing people of the world, chuckle at a mention of purgatory. Rich and wicked families, hopefully, are the only victims of this scam. But if honest, humble Christians are blackmailed to pay at a time of bereavement, hell is in session, not purgatory.

We Have Found Our Loved Ones
Chapter XV

No one who believes in prayer thinks physics can limit it. Mystical communication to a far way God is the way most people think of it. If prayer were that, we might indeed pray to the saints. Fortunately, blessedly, we do not have to understand prayer to benefit from it. The time has come to reveal ubiquity and its implication for prayer.

Roman Catholicism is the test case. How can this be explained in a compassionate way?

Squeaketh the mouse, "You? Compassionate? Ha."

What if this realization is traumatic? What if they howl? What if they are truly hurt in their hearts? What if they fall to the ground and weep?

What if a billion Christians have a temper tantrum? Temper tantrums do occur in religion. An example is in Acts 19:23-41. Here is a quick skim through it.

> A silversmith who made silver shrines for Diana...called craftsmen together... you all realize how our prosperity depends on this particular work... this man Paul has succeeded in changing the minds... Paul himself wanted to go in among the crowd, but the disciples would not allow him... A man called Alexander whom the Jews put forward was pushed into the forefront of the crowd... he tried to make a speech of defense to the people. But as soon as they realized that he was a Jew they shouted as one man for about two hours, 'Great is Diana of the Ephesians!'

The rage at Ephesus was a powerful devotion to little silver idols. The religious experience of humanity includes many rages like the rage at Ephesus. It was very religious. Rage by a billion Christians is possible. We can avoid that.

The question arises, do the prayers of Christians to Christian saints have a better chance than the prayers of pagans to pagan gods? Its like a child talking to a picture of someone compared to a child talking to a cartoon character. Neither is a problem, and neither is an actual communication.

I visualize a Christian finally meeting the Christian saint and asking, "Why didn't you answer my prayers?" The saint, aghast, replies, "Prayers to me? You dummkopf!" In fact, St. Mary, the mother of Jesus has not actually heard a single one of the lengthy prayers of the trillion aimed at her from the people of Earth. God would not allow her to be tormented so. Paradise is paradise. All the hundred-trillion Hail-Marys went nowhere. She does love us and prays for us, but her bliss has not been disturbed by direct messages from Earth.

Much effort was expended through the centuries to devise just the right prayer to just the right saint.

Squeaketh the mouse, "I'll need three St. Christopher medals. Don't tell anyone."

None of these tearful prayers traveled upward by a millimeter. The question is, are Roman Catholics who only pray to saints entirely without benefit of prayer? Official liturgies contain prayers to God. Those would suffice, but what if those prayers are skipped (or demoted below the saints)? And anyway, what happened to the safe harbor of prayer?

Not to worry. "We do not know what we should pray for as we ought, but the Spirit Himself makes intercession for us with groanings which cannot be uttered." — Romans 8:26 (proving safe harbor). You see, we, all of us, are of the fallen human race, so we actually need God to pray for us, and, amazingly, He does. And this never changes. These prayers are always perfect, efficacious, and saving. Even the deepest, silliest saint-clinger benefits from secret intercessory prayers made by the Holy Ghost. This is indeed fortunate for them and for us. So, rejoice always with the saints, but do not pray to them. You will not run afoul of Romans 1:25, “Who changed the truth of God into a lie and worshipped and served the creature more than the Creator.”

I have opened before you, and I hope you will have accepted, great familiarity with the saints. In view of which, I had a duty to explain that premature communication to them would be bad. Communication with us is the job of the angels who visit our locations. We have the saints, we know the saints, we love the saints, the saints love us, but communication would be premature. We always have their good will without asking. Did we ask for their prayers that are reported to us in Revelation 6:10, “And they cried with a loud voice, saying, ‘How long, O Lord, holy and true, dost Thou not judge and avenge our blood on them that dwell on the earth?’ ” We did not ask before that event, but we have the good intercession of the saints anyway.

What if the best person you know exclusively prays to Mary? What if the best person in town exclusively prays to Mary? What if the best Christian on earth exclusively prays to Mary? This requires an explanation. I have one, but let’s first ask the ultimate question.

Question: What about those who prayed to saints and then became holy martyrs?

Answer: They are indeed holy, but that does not prove doctrine. Nor can you prove a doctrine by giving up your body to be burned. Nor can any other thing about one's life prove doctrine. This is why St. Paul warned so strenuously against false apostles in 2 Corinthians 11:13-15. They presented themselves so well that they seemed more genuine than Paul, then easily subverted Church doctrine. This is a continuing problem throughout Church history.

Here is Luther's theory as to how we should treat supposed new doctrines. It is extremely skeptical.

> There are two kinds of doctrine. The first one is already received and confirmed by divine authority or miracles. Against this kind no miracles are to be granted, not even an angel from heaven (Gal. 1:8). The second kind of doctrine is still to be received. Here one should not believe unless signs are done, since God never spoke a new Word which He did not confirm with signs. Thus He confirmed the Law of Moses with very great signs; the Gospel also, when it was first received, with very great and almost continual ones. Therefore when a new doctrine comes, its acceptance is to be suspended until signs occur. If we do this, God is faithful and will not permit them (that is, the false prophets) to do signs.
>
> *((Also, "God never spoke a new Word which He did not confirm with signs."*
> *Martin Luther, Luther's Works, Vol. 9: Lectures on Deuteronomy, ed. Jaroslav Jan Pelikan, Hilton C. Oswald, and Helmut T. Lehmann, vol. 9 (Saint Louis: Concordia Publishing House, 1999), 188.))*

Again, nothing about the life of a lone, saintly person on Earth tips the scale towards proving doctrine, absent miracles. My understanding of Luther's statement is that the final authority is Scripture, but without starting from scratch as I, in my fundamentalist period, obstinately did. Luther did not start from scratch. Luther had all the Catholic achievements as a resource, and he changed as little as possible. Applying "only scripture" to knock off a few barnacles from that ancient statue, the Catholic Church, he made it far more beautiful. He was not ungrateful for the received standard theology and made maximum use of it, even though the contemporary church administration of his time was trying to kill him.

Time to provide a key to understanding those who prayed to saints and then became holy martyrs. We are blessed, indeed, that God has granted us a safe harbor in prayer and prays for us in our stead. You see, there are so very many that pray to saints. And they are so very repetitive, with more prayers offered to saints than to God. Here is how that is calculated. Half of the 1.3 billion Roman Catholics pray times 59 rosary beads times half of the beads times an average of one prayer session per week times 52 weeks per year = (1/2)*1,300,000,000*59*(1/2)*(1)*52= 997.1 billion Hail Mary's alone. This is compared to half pray of 3 billion other God-fearing persons times one prayer session per week times

52 weeks per year = (1/2)*3,000,000,000*(1)*52 = just 78 billion prayers. This ratio of more than 12 to 1 will hold, as prayer sessions for each group are increased or decreased. I conclude that Hail Mary's alone greatly outnumber all prayers to God. This is not a problem, since those prayers go nowhere.

Even though this is shocking, even though by its sheer weight it might be considered a serious error—by which I mean sin—we should not fret. The manifold grace of God transforms our world and this issue. Safe harbor holds. Even the prayers of great theologians are ignorant and need safe harbor. It is good that we now have wisdom with respect to this issue. And, let us not allow this issue to harm our Christian fellowship. Although, if someone who prays to the saints lords it over someone who refuses to, that… that should make us sad.

And now for Stupidity No. 3 about God. All my views on praying to the saints can be ignored except one. Worst of all, some teach that Jesus is a stern judge and an angry God, justifying prayers to saints as sweet intercessors. A Roman Catholic theologian and venerated saint wrote,

> Behold how Christ chides, censures, and condemns the Pharisees so harshly throughout the Gospel, whereas the Virgin Mary is always kind and gentle and never utters an unfriendly word.

Another former Catholic wrote,

> **From this he [the venerated Saint] inferred: 'Christ is given to scolding and punishing, but Mary has nothing but sweetness and love.' Therefore, Christ was generally feared; we fled from Him and took refuge with the saints, calling upon Mary and others to deliver us from our distress. We regarded them all as holier than Christ. Christ was only the executioner, while the saints were our mediators.**

The former Catholic was *really* a "former Catholic." In other words, it was Martin Luther, and the venerated Saint was Bernard. *(((Luther, M. (1999, c1957). Vol. 22: Luther's works, vol. 22: Sermons on the Gospel of St. John: Chapters 1-4 (J. J. Pelikan, H. C. Oswald & H. T. Lehmann, Ed.). Luther's Works (Jn 3:20). Saint Louis: Concordia Publishing House.)))*

(((Note in Luther's Works: Luther seems to be thinking of statements by Bernard like that in In Nativitate Beatae Mariae Virginis Sermo, Patrologia, Series Latina, CLXXXIII, 441.)))

Luther claims that Bernard did something of the utmost importance near the end of his life,

> **He hung his cowl on the wall and prayed: 'God's Son had a twofold claim to heaven: in the first place, as the Son of God, by inheritance, He was born to the kingdom of heaven; in the second place, He has also gained heaven. And since this was entirely unnecessary for Him, He transferred this right to me, which I must appropriate by faith.' O, St. Bernard, that was a timely return!**
>
> *(((A note in Luther's Works, Vol. 21: Luther, M. (1999, c1956). Vol. 21: Luther's works, vol. 21: The Sermon on the Mount and the Magnificat*

(J. J. Pelikan, H. C. Oswald & H. T. Lehmann, Ed.). Luther's Works. Saint Louis: Concordia Publishing House.)))

(((Also, Luther often quoted Bernard saying, "Oh, I have lived damnably and passed my life shamefully!" According to a note in Luther's Works, Vol. 21: Luther often quoted these words of Bernard; cf. Luther's Works, 12, 335. The words appear in Bernard's " Sermones in Cantica, " Sermon XX, Patrologia, Series Latina, CLXXXIII, 867.)))

The wonderfully sweet saving faith in Jesus Christ that Bernard found at the end of his life was a full repudiation of Stupidity No. 3 about God, the former view both monks, Bernard and Luther, had held. I do not know which of St. Bernard's views, the former or the latter, is taught today as his. Surely, as regards doctrinal views, it is mainly his views at the end of his life that should be taught as, "St. Bernard."

Here is Luther's description of himself as a monk.

> I myself was a monk for twenty years. I tortured myself with prayers, fasting, vigils, and freezing; the frost alone might have killed me. It caused me pain such as I will never inflict on myself again, even if I could. What else did I seek by doing this but God, who was supposed to note my strict observance of the monastic order and my austere life? I constantly walked in a dream and lived in real idolatry. For I did not believe in Christ; I regarded Him only as a severe and terrible Judge, portrayed as seated on a rainbow. Therefore I cast about for other intercessors, Mary and various other saints, also my own works and the merits of my order. And I did all this for the sake of God, not for money or goods.

Nevertheless, this was heresy and idolatry, since I did not know Christ and did not seek in and through Him what I wanted.

(((Martin Luther, Luther's Works, Vol. 24: Sermons on the Gospel of St. John: Chapters 14-16, ed. Jaroslav Jan Pelikan, Hilton C. Oswald, and Helmut T. Lehmann, vol. 24 (Saint Louis: Concordia Publishing House, 1999), 23–24.)))

In reference to "I judge no man"—John 8:15, Luther wrote this: The preachers who thus perverted Christ for us were the penalty for our great ingratitude. They converted light into darkness and changed Christ from a Savior into a tyrant and judge.

This beautiful text bids us not to picture Christ as a judge. The pope, however, emphasized Christ as the Judge on the Last Day. The papists imagine that Christ sits enthroned above just for the purpose of judging and condemning. That is the picture I had of Christ, and you cannot deny that it was also your conception of Christ in the papacy. This image of Christ gave rise to all the good works, cloisters, and monastic orders, with which the Judge is to be reconciled. Then also Mary's help was invoked, who was to show Christ her breasts as a reminder [What?].

In that way the Gospel was thoroughly destroyed and exterminated, and we became genuinely hostile to Christ. I would gladly have seen Christ vanish from the scene. Everyone fled from Him and became His enemy.

(((Martin Luther, Luther's Works, Vol. 23: Sermons on the Gospel of St. John: Chapters 6-8, ed. Jaroslav Jan Pelikan, Hilton C. Oswald, and Helmut T. Lehmann, vol. 23 (Saint Louis: Concordia Publishing House, 1999), 335-336.)))

I would be glad if I were found to be wrong about Roman Catholic practice in these times, very glad to be very wrong.

Oh. Did "Invictus" survive? Invincible free will should expect to have many battles, wounds, bandages, and bruises. It surely does, but the Lord's will is perfect. There can be only one, invincible, free will, the will of the one omnipotent, omnipresent God. So, "Invictus" is false, but that is wonderful for us. Do not despair. In the safe harbor of prayer, "Invictus" becomes a prayer, or it always was. It says, "I thank whatever gods." "Invictus" is non-specific, so it would include the true God. For this reason, it excels even prayers to Mary because a prayer to Mary is specific without including the true God. Both faulty prayers are nothing, of course. But both are in the safe harbor. There you have it, the Lord Himself hath made intercession for us, pouring grace upon grace.

We have proven the Protestant view. I also conclude that praying to the saints is geometrically stupid, theologically stupid, and ill mannered. But, with the idea of a safe harbor, we have developed a benign form of the Protestant view. Roman Catholics are far too intelligent, lovely, and well-mannered toward holy things for the worst (Stupidity No. 3 about God) to continue. But don't tell them. I wash my hands of this mess.

Squeaketh the mouse, "I declare absolution for all those who pray to the saints and the entire forgiveness of all their sins, unless they make Jesus a severe and terrible Judge."

We Have Found Our Loved Ones
Chapter XVI

Oh, but don't we need intercession? Even though it seems wise to do so, many God-fearing people never consider intercessory prayer by any one at all. On the other hand, many do seek that, and they are probably wiser. We can hope they are not praying to and asking the saints in heaven to be the intercessors.

I found a surprise as I explored the plain teaching of Jesus on an individual's power of prayer. Many times, I have heard this passage read in church, and have read it myself, but I missed the point.

> Hitherto you have not asked any thing in my name. Ask, and you shall receive; that your joy may be full. These things I have spoken to you in proverbs. The hour cometh, when I will no more speak to you in proverbs, but will shew you plainly of the Father. In that day you shall ask in my name; and I say not to you, that I will ask the Father for you: For the Father himself loveth you, because you have loved me, and have believed that I came out from God. – John 16:24-27 Catholic Bible

(Note that "I came out from God" supports ubiquity and Virgin Birth; these were studied earlier.)

In fewer than one hundred words, Jesus issues an invitation to any Christian to personally connect with infinite power. I think many others must have noticed this, but I missed it entirely.

This connection I take to be momentary because of the term, "in my name." In Christ a Christian is cleansed, again and again, for we are sinners. Momentarily perfected in Christ, it is safe for one to appear before infinite power, wisdom, and goodness. Otherwise, it would not be safe.

The statement, "I say not unto you, that I will pray the Father for you: For the Father himself loveth you," proves that you do not need an intercessor. And this is true in all circumstances, as St. Paul expresses.

> Therefore let us [with privilege] approach the throne of grace [that is, the throne of God's gracious favor] with confidence and without fear, so that we may receive mercy [for our failures] and find [His amazing] grace to help in time of need [an appropriate blessing, coming just at the right moment].
>
> – Hebrews 4:16
>
> *brackets and italics are according to the Amplified Bible.*

To visualize this privilege, I now advance an image that I call, "the Escalator." Think of an up-escalator that goes through the roof; it is stopped. You kneel and pray on the steps; you close your eyes. The escalator silently starts and takes you beyond the roof. Your eyes are still closed, and you do not perceive it. The escalator reverses and brings you back. The escalator stops. You stand up and walk away, not knowing that you visited an awesome elevation. Suppose also that all this could happen at heaven's speed, that is, in the blink of an eye, in a millisecond.

This image fits. Jesus is the ladder or escalator or the Escalator. I propose the Escalator as either a physical analogy to teach a spiritual principle or even as literally physical. There are many physical analogies with spiritual principles like sowing and reaping, the mustard seed, lost sheep, etc. On the other hand, we may ask, "Could the Escalator be literal?" or "How literal could it be?"

As He taught about prayer, Jesus said He would show us the Father. "In my name" was used twice. If "in" includes the geometric meaning of being inside the Son of God, as with Baptism and the Lord's Supper, then any common prayer could also include "Real Presence," even the real presence of God the Father. He is everywhere all the time, but to officially meet Him would be a Real Presence. But you already knew that; you already believed, without any help from me, that God is really present during prayer.

Squeaketh the mouse, "I already knew that."

In this Bible passage, no intercessor prays for you. The supplicant, that's you, comes before God the Father in prayer. The Lord's Prayer is a frequent example, and there is more. Comparing the passages, Matthew 6:1-15 (where Jesus taught us the Lord's Prayer) and His teaching in John 16:24-27 (above), these pair up well. In John, the invisible is described, and in Matthew, Jesus functioned visibly as a teacher taking us to the Father. It is not a prayer to a far-away god; you have no power to do that. It is a meeting with God the Father; you are granted this access by Jesus. We know not where this happens, at your location or in the air or in heaven. Regardless of where, this is a real meeting. That's the simplest explanation of Jesus' words.

We should be able to determine if a popular prayer fits within the teaching of Jesus in John 16:24-27. We will use the Prayer to St. Michael the Archangel as an example.

> Prayer to St. Michael the Archangel
> St. Michael the Archangel,
> defend us in battle.
> Be our defense against the wickedness and snares of the Devil.
> May God rebuke him, we humbly pray,
> and do thou,
> O Prince of the heavenly hosts,
> by the power of God,

thrust into hell Satan,
and all the evil spirits,
who prowl about the world
seeking the ruin of souls. Amen.
O glorious prince St. Michael,
chief and commander of the heavenly hosts,
guardian of souls, vanquisher of rebel spirits,
servant in the house of the Divine King
and our admirable conductor,
you who shine with excellence
and superhuman virtue deliver us from all evil,
who turn to you with confidence
and enable us by your gracious protection
to serve God more and more faithfully every day.

(((As found at Prayer to St. Michael the Archangel | EWTN; https://www.ewtn.com/catholicism/devotions/prayer-to-st-michael-the-archangel-371

The italicized material was added by the Eternal Word Television Network (EWTN) website. EWTN bills itself as the Global Catholic Network.)))

Analysis:

1. Does it address God the Father? No.
2. Does it even address God? No.
3. Does it ask in the name of Jesus? No.
4. Is it dualistic? Yes. But Jesus' prayer instructions are not dualistic in the slightest. Recall that in religion, dualism is anything similar to a good god and an evil god fighting it out.

5. Does this prayer suppose a human power that we do not have? Yes. We have no power to communicate to an angel that is not touching us or nearby.

6. Does it acknowledge the love of God? No. Jesus' instructions emphasize that love.

7. Does it acknowledge ubiquity like Jesus' instructions and the Lord's Prayer? No.

8. Should this prayer be judged as a total loss? Well, actually, it's not a total loss. In the safe harbor of prayer, this prayer goes nowhere, but the Holy Spirit may make intercession to God. Grace prevents the Prayer to St. Michael the Archangel from being a total loss.

9. The problem here is not about St. Michael, just the notion of praying to him. The Church of England, Lutheranism, and other Protestant groups have Michael on the Church Calendar for recognition. Every part of the Christian Church loves this archangel. The source has a paragraph of praise after the "Amen." This praise is well stated.

10. This completes the analysis of the Prayer to St. Michael the Archangel.

Back to intercession. There are intercessions and intercessors, even within the Trinity. Jesus did it (Luke 22:32) and the Holy Spirit continues to do it (Romans 8:26-27). Intercessions by created beings occur in all circumstances, too. But this passage has no intercessor (unless you intercede for others). In fact, with the words, "I say not unto you, that I will pray the Father for you," the passage specifically takes our focus away from intercession. When does it apply? What does it advise? Clearly, the most important case is when someone thinks they need an intercessor. In such a case, they need the very best advice possible, which Jesus has provided. He directes away from relying on an intercessor and strongly advises simple prayer itself because of its mighty power.

The thought occurs that a time of desperation is the occasion described as, "the time cometh, when I shall no more speak unto you in proverbs, but I shall shew you plainly of the Father." At such a moment of need, you shall have an audience with the Creator.

The time had come for Jesus to reveal to the Disciples their relationship to God the Father, saying, "I shall shew you plainly of the Father. At that day ye shall ask in my name." Thus, the teaching is that prayer is so important that the supplicant should pray, even if it seems that one cannot. One must summon up, that is, be granted this faith. Faith is bolstered by the promise, "ask, and ye shall receive." This passage is an endowment of mighty power. The power flows to those who have true faith, "because ye have loved me, and have believed that I came out from God."

OK, we find this to be difficult. It's like the mystery of repentance. I must repent to receive faith, but I must have faith to repent; it's a conundrum. Do you remember another Bible conundrum?

> Then said Jesus unto his disciples, Verily I say unto you, That a rich man shall hardly enter into the kingdom of heaven. And again I say unto you, It is easier for a camel to go

> through the eye of a needle, than for a rich man to enter into the kingdom of God. When his disciples heard it, they were exceedingly amazed, saying, Who then can be saved? But Jesus beheld them, and said unto them, With men this is impossible; but with God all things are possible. —Matthew 19:23-26

I have yet to state that "God does it all." When some people hear that God did everything concerning their salvation, they become angry. But in this passage, God is the only solution. It is a question of means, meaning wealth. Jesus, a man of the building trade, a carpenter was, as I reason it, of the lower middle class. It seems that He chose Disciples from there and upward. Because the Disciples knew they were much better off than the humble poor, Jesus' words brought them up short. They wondered, "Who then can be saved?" It was a perfect opportunity for Jesus to tell them and us, "God does it all." That, of course, is the meaning of "elect," that we studied earlier. Jesus described an impossibility; then He said, "With God all things are possible."

Getting back to prayer, we find that to be a conundrum also. Jesus taught that earnest prayers are powerful and sufficient. His statements about prayer leave us feeling as though we have no faith at all. I ask, "Where are we going to get that kind of faith?" Answer: God does it all.

> For this reason I am telling you, whatever things you ask for in prayer [in accordance with God's will], believe [with confident trust] that you have received them, and they will be given to you. —Mark 11:24 Amplified Bible

And Jesus expects you to believe that just a few earnest prayers (maybe just one) are, nevertheless, sufficient.

> But when ye pray, use not vain repetitions, as the heathen do: for they think that they shall be heard for their much speaking. —Matthew 6:7

The sufficiency of earnest prayer makes sense if there is Real Presence in prayer. When you have been heard in heaven's highest court, that is sufficient.

It is important to be wise or at least not be ridiculous. A proper understanding of a great parable will help us to somehow believe in prayer's sufficiency.

> Then He spoke a parable to them, that men always ought to pray and not lose heart, saying: "There was in a certain city a judge who did not fear God nor regard man. Now there was a widow in that city; and she came to him, saying, Get justice for me from my adversary. And he would not for a while; but afterward he said within himself, Though I do not fear God nor regard man, yet because this widow troubles me I will avenge her, lest by her continual coming she weary me. Then the Lord said, Hear what the unjust judge said.

> And shall God not avenge His own elect who cry out day and night to Him, though He bears long with them? I tell you that He will avenge them speedily. Nevertheless, when the Son of Man comes, will He really find faith on the earth?
> – Luke 18:1-8 New King James Version

It would be a great misunderstanding to think that God is like the unjust judge, or that He therefore requires much repetition. Much repetition has already been rejected. No, the final sentence reveals that the key is faith. This passage was to help the Disciples have faith that their prayers would be efficacious.

Squeaketh the mouse, "Effie K. She us. Got it."

Intercessory prayers should, therefore, be the entourage for your own prayer, not its substitute. Amazingly, intercession by the clergy, priest, prayer group, bishop, angels, the Pope, the saints in heaven, and, dare I say, the Son of God and the Holy Ghost, pale in comparison to your own supplication. Now you know power. This power is placed on you like an inherited crown; you did nothing to gain it.

This is the main message. You did not request this great power; it is placed upon you by direction of God. Jesus revealed you to yourself. You, in heaven, are someone who can bring a case to that court. You do not have to get special permission to do that. You have general permission because of Jesus.

Therefore, although finding an intercessor can be comforting; it is never a necessity. Simple slogan: "Intercession has its place, but it is not first place."

Squeaketh the mouse, "Oh gag. Not a slogan."

It looks too difficult, but Jesus would not mislead us. Even though we seem totally ill equipped to pray in the way that Jesus taught, somehow, we can. If I am thinking about myself, I will never have the courage to pray as Christ teaches. Maybe I can follow Luther's leadership here.

> **With my works I will never induce God to speak to me** and enlighten me, but the Father sends the Son and speaks of the Son. He illumines me through this light, so that I recognize Christ. Thus our salvation is to be attributed solely to the Son; and the glory belongs to the Father, who speaks of the Son through the Son. My good works are not to merit eternal life for me.
>
> *(((Luther, M. (1999, c1959). Vol. 23: Luther's works, vol. 23: Sermons on the Gospel of St. John: Chapters 6-8 (J. J. Pelikan, H. C. Oswald & H. T. Lehmann, Ed.). Luther's Works (Jn 6:51). Saint Louis: Concordia Publishing House.)))*

So, instead of thinking of myself, I must lift my heart. To do that, what shall be my meditation?

> **A single work of Christ excels the works of all men**, and I would rather call one work of Christ my own than all the works and holiness of all the saints. What is

man compared with God, or a human work compared with divine works? Christ's works are divine works, but our works are human works.

(((Martin Luther, Luther's Works, Vol. 23: Sermons on the Gospel of St. John: Chapters 6-8, ed. Jaroslav Jan Pelikan, Hilton C. Oswald, and Helmut T. Lehmann, vol. 23 (Saint Louis: Concordia Publishing House, 1999), 182.)))

Thus, by not thinking of myself but only the works of Christ, I could become well prepared to pray according to the revelation in John 16:24-27. It is an aid to prayer, and the Stations of the Cross is such an aid. It doesn't matter if it is formulaic. Many recitations are formulaic ways of thinking aright, such as the Lord's Prayer or the Twenty-third Psalm. Not that they are magic, but they are very helpful, especially before prayer. Hosea 14:2 recommends this, "Take with you words, and turn to the Lord." Certainly, authentic prayer is not limited to what is spontaneous.

Scriptural Way of the Cross or Biblical Stations of the Cross Introduced by Pope John Paul II

1. Jesus in the Garden of Gethsemane ....Matthew 26:36-41
2. Jesus is betrayed by Judas and arrested .... Mark 14:43-46
3. Jesus is condemned by the Sanhedrin.......................... Luke 22:66-71
4. Jesus is denied by St. Peter ....Matthew 26:69-75
5. Jesus is judged by Pontius Pilate ....Mark 15:1-5, 15
6. Jesus is scourged at the pillar and crowned with thorns ....John 19:1-3

7. Jesus Bears the Cross ....John 19:6, 15-17

8. Jesus is helped by Simon the Cyrenian to carry the cross.....Mark 15:21

9. Jesus meets the women of Jerusalem ....Luke 23:27-31

10. Jesus is crucified.. Luke 23:33-34

11. Jesus promises his kingdom to the good thief .... Luke 23:39-43

12. Jesus speaks to his mother and the beloved disciple .... John 19:25-27

13. Jesus dies on the cross... Luke 23:44-46

14. Jesus is placed in the tomb.....................................Matthew 27:57-60

(((http://www.joyfulheart.com/stations-of-the-cross/scriptural-way-of-the-cross.htm)))

What have we just accomplished? In this chapter we discussed access to infinite power. It is a topic worthy of study forever, that is, in this life and the next. Based on Jesus words, this approach to prayer is destined to bring success.

In the previous chapter, we found praying to the saints, in and of itself, had zero power. I did acknowledge that within the grace of the safe harbor of prayer, even the most insane of prayers could be somewhat beneficial. Even with that, the contrast between these modes of prayer is like comparing a thimble with the universe. Prayers to the saints go nowhere, so not even a thimble full of power accessed. But, sometimes, people who get everything wrong, have success anyway.

In any case, we succeed with God's help.

We Have Found Our Loved Ones
Chapter XVII

Wonderful conclusion: We did it.

We did not just find the simplest geometry. We found all the saints. Our loved ones are among them, as fellow saints. Their bliss we have tasted. It is a good achievement, and it is also good that we are wise enough to be able to handle this knowledge. We have not contradicted the Bible. And, amazingly, we have not contradicted geometry or the science of physics.

Sometimes the saints are on the far side of the universe. Sometimes they are close by and just above us. We comprehend their status and ours. We are united with the saints; and yet communication with them is without a practical pathway from the Earth. What makes that the case? What is that perfect barrier? Is it distance? As we have seen, distance is not always the barrier. That perfect barrier is the will of God.

We have found our loved ones. God makes marvelous provision for them as they tour paradise. It is only on Earth that we cry, "My God, my God, why hast thou forsaken me?" Nothing on Earth compares to the glory granted to the saints. They and we are the inheritors of all things. We have found them and even tasted of their glory. They travel about enjoying all of Heaven, which includes all the fullness of the universe. Their movement in Heaven is instant, effortless, easy, satisfying, beautiful, rich, blissful, varied, restful, exciting, opulent, luxurious, joyful, musical, dynamic, bejeweled, crowned, and royal, because God personally provides for all their needs, wants, and desires. The universe is the city of the living God.

Squeaketh the mouse, "Don't forget delicious."

We have this knowledge as a gift, a gift that heaven has given us. We did not climb our way upward to attain this knowledge. This knowledge was destined to come down to earth. "When he ascended up on high, he led captivity captive, and gave gifts unto men." —Ephesians 4:8 KJV. And "A man cannot receive any thing, unless it be given him from heaven." —John 3:27 Catholic Bible. Luther has, "A man cannot take anything unless it is given him from heaven." We had no power to rise up and yank this knowledge down from heaven. It had to be brought down to us, even if it seems that we have done nothing more than use a little reasoning.

What we have not learned is far more important than what we

have learned. God could have made the universe a trillion times bigger or placed it on the head of a pin. The real question is not about heaven and earth and their uses by anybody, even God. The real question is, why? Why did God create sentient beings with free will, or seeming free will, such that they could fall? Why did He interact with them in a highly varied list of ways? These ways include, teacher, judge, executioner, companion, helper, and deliverer, all indicating ubiquity.

The most astonishing role was as blood sacrifice. Our minds, even though we have stretched them, cannot comprehend a role for which there is no rational explanation. Grasping for one, for an understanding of heroism itself, a reward for one's cause is considered,

> **For the joy set before him he endured the cross, scorning its shame, and sat down at the right hand of the throne of God. – Hebrews 12:2**

It fits well that the greatest sacrifice of all, earns the greatest reward of all. A reward for His cause, that is His people, is an aspect of His sacrifice. But such heroism is a "single," versus the "double" in the quote from St. Bernard which I repeat,

> **God's Son had a twofold claim to heaven: in the first place, as the Son of God, by inheritance, He was born to the kingdom of heaven; in the second place, He has also gained**

heaven. And since this was entirely unnecessary for Him, He transferred this right to me, which I must appropriate by faith.

Bernard insists that Christ already had the most royal title, but independently of His title he took on the role of one who had no title and won it a second way. During His earthly sojourn He was, let's say, a man not of the higher classes, or He was even a despised and untouchable (because of rumors he was illegitimate). He performed the heroism to gain the victory. For Himself "this was entirely unnecessary," but for love's sake, He laid down His life.

> No man taketh it from me, but I lay it down of myself. I have power to lay it down, and I have power to take it again. This commandment have I received of my Father. – John 10:18

St. Bernard did not exaggerate as he expressed this, "He transferred this right to me, which I must appropriate by faith."

> Greater love hath no man than this, that a man lay down his life for his friends. Ye are my friends, if ye do whatsoever I command you. Henceforth I call you not servants; for the servant knoweth not what his lord doeth: but I have called you friends; for all things that I have heard of my Father I have made known unto you – John 15:13

I, despite being the most blessed person on the earth, am so little. I am least of all. It is not that I have happened upon this or developed this study on my own. Surely an angel helps me, like Daniel 9:22. I choose the Literal Standard Version for that verse, which, more than others, places it in the present. Angels are trying to increase our understanding and devils darken it; this applies to every individual right now.

> And he gives understanding, and speaks with me, and says, O Daniel, now I have come forth to cause you to consider understanding wisely.

I hope you benefited from our travels.

Fare thee well.

Squeaketh the mouse, "Fare thee well."

> "Giving thanks unto the Father, which hath made us meet to be partakers of the inheritance of the saints in light."
> – Colossians 1:12

Don't Answer the Door

At this point the Jehovah's Witnesses knocked on my door (really).

Squeaketh the mouse, "Don't open it!"

They explained that I could live forever on the earth. Having completed this study, I had been thinking of much grander glory than that. Living forever on earth sounded awful. They buttressed their claim using their spiffy new app for smartphones. You could tell that the earth was their hope by the way their faces glowed as they shared their message.

In response, a person (your servant) waved at the sky, claiming that billions of saints dwell throughout the universe and more.

Squeaketh the mouse, "They look at you like you're crazy."

I mentioned Deuteronomy 4:32, where Moses dared the people, "ask from the one side of heaven unto the other."

Squeaketh the mouse, "Didn't help."

I recalled that the number 144,000 is pivotal for them because they think heaven is limited to that number (based on Revelation 7:4). I told them that all the numbers in the Bible are figurative.

Squeaketh the mouse, "Didn't help."

I was losing. I told them that the heavens are a tent to dwell in (from Isaiah 40:22).

Squeaketh the mouse, "Give up."

I gave up.

I did tell them that when (not if) they get "disfellowshipped" to come and see me. Disfellowshipped means kicked out of the Jehovah's Witnesses.

Squeaketh the mouse, "Is that better?"

I have cult experience.

Squeaketh the mouse, "I can believe that."

Exiting the cult was good for St. Augustine, who left Manichaeism; good for St. Bernard, who late in life, hung his monk's cowl on the wall and sweetly depended on faith only; good for Martin Luther the Reformer, who shook world; and good for me.

Squeaketh the mouse, "But what have you really accomplished?"

If there is any value to this experience (and there may not be), it certainly reveals two extreme points of view. My geometric point of view may glorify God more than any other view.

Get Martin Luther

On Dec. 31, 2004, I purchased a CD_ROM; it is now out of date. Here is what was written on the package: “Luther's Works on CD ROM: 55 Volume American Edition CD-ROM – January 1, 2004, by Martin Luther (Author), Jaroslav Pelikan (Editor), Helmut T Lehmann (Editor).” It worked on every version of the Windows operating system until June 15, 2022. On that date Microsoft killed it by killing the Internet Explorer browser. (Tears.) I used the software for over 900 weekly sessions of at least two hours, over 17 years. Few pieces of software have continued to work that well that long. The cost works out to 2½ cents per day. Not that I am cheap.

The best things in life are free; reading Luther was almost free. Education is rarely this much fun. It bathed me in fascination, discovery, satisfaction, and joy. You see, it is a special experience to walk with Luther as he solves mystery after mystery. And here is the very best part: reading Luther was never vexing and often humorous. Luther delivers or the Holy Spirit delivers spiritual sustenance through Luther. That is why I recommend Luther. I do not recommend books about Luther; I recommend Luther. I do not even read the General Introductions or the Volume Introductions; I go right to Luther. I hope you want to test this by reading some Luther for himself.

The CD_ROM software no longer works, so here is how to get Luther.

Fortunately, Logos Bible Software is available from logos.com as a replacement. As I write this, https://www.logos.com/product/15485/luthers-works states, "Now, Logos Bible Software has partnered with Fortress Press and Concordia Publishing House to offer the entire 55-volume set of Luther's Works for download." Good. But when it comes time for you to buy the 55-volume set, don't. Do not jump in and buy anything online assuming you will get the right product. Contact a Logos Bible Software – Direct Sales Representative. There are many products online, some of them thousands of dollars. Getting the right product will be impossible without directions from a Direct Sales Representative. Currently (summer of 2022) the price is $259.00, which is a one-time charge.

If you are not ready for that, a free resource is available at https://www.logos.com/basic

The library that installs with Logos Basic includes the one book that I hope you will read next, "Luther's Commentary on Galatians." The Bible, the Confessions of St. Augustine, and dozens of other books are included for free, but Luther's Galatians (its name in English history) is the treasure. By reading it, you will know whether Luther is for you.

In the full 55-volume set, Luther's Galatians is Volume 26. The sequence I recommend for reading should start at Volume 25, "Luther's commentary on Romans." So, if you have already read Luther's Galatians in Logos Basic and later buy the 55 volumes, I recommend the following: Read Volume 25, Luther's Commentary on Romans, then do 27-30, and then 1-24. All 55 reside on your laptop or other device. You do not need an internet connection except during installation. You know how to get Luther. Again, I do not recommend that a reader start at Volume 1; skip over to Volume 25, read through 30, and then read 1 through 24.

Get Music

Luther was musical and made contributions to music, but I am not talking about that. I am talking about the sort of music that helps most people study. It might be instrumental music, not necessarily religious. First, I want to tell you about a music show that you cannot get. I speak of "Baroque around the Clock" from "AVRO Klassiek Baroque Around The Clock, Classical radio. Hilversum, Netherlands." It has been gone many years. It had the advantage of a great selection of baroque music, 24/7; and, best of all, the talking was in Dutch, which does not distract because I cannot understand a word of it. In my opinion, it set the standard for music that was helpful for reading Luther but not distracting.

There is plenty of music on the internet, 24/7. Consider, "Sunday Baroque" from sundaybaroque.org or WSHU Public Radio, "Pipedreams" from NPR, or "With Heart and Voice" from WXXI Classical Public Radio. You can play the latest shows (perhaps a week late) anytime. There are many other possibilities, Youtube, Pandora, etc. These are dependent on having internet, but terrestrial radio is not. If you are lucky, you have a classical music station. Best possibility is your own CD collection.

There are many other possibilities, and music may or may not be helpful.

Do We Need An Underground Church In America?

I am not talking about Luther's statement, "If it were not for persecution, we would be as bad and base as our adversaries." I am certainly not seeking a spiritual benefit from being persecuted. Hopefully, this is just a thought experiment.

(((Martin Luther, Luther's Works, Vol. 23: Sermons on the Gospel of St. John: Chapters 6-8, ed. Jaroslav Jan Pelikan, Hilton C. Oswald, and Helmut T. Lehmann, vol. 23 (Saint Louis: Concordia Publishing House, 1999), 7.)))

We observe that far away Christians, Jews, and other religious innocents endure persecution and martyrdom. I am focusing on the Church, but the reasoning would apply to any harmless, ethical, persecuted religious believers by substituting terminology. For instance, a group that seems to qualify is the Falun Gong (see Wikipedia). We know that such groups need their churches and their lives to be protected or even kept secret. If we solve the problem of how to be a Christian under a deep level of secrecy, we will solve all.

Suppose we want to read something regularly in secret, leaving no trace. People all over the world are seeking ways to do that, and failing. This is especially true in China, and there are other examples. You would not be able to outsmart a nation state. These are the threats: overbearing government's hatred of Christianity, hostile religious authority, violent popular prejudice, or even close family relations who are actual threats (I refer to honor killings, see Wikipedia). A possible solution is that you should be able to accomplish secret study in a private residence. What follows will help you do exactly that.

Faced with the need for confidentiality, we desire to know what can be done easily and economically. Bible reading on computers has been around for decades. This largely solves the problem. Reading can be done without paper bibles, books, or tracts trafficked or lying around. Seems perfect.

An extra level of secrecy can be achieved using a virtual machine. A virtual machine (VM) is all software; it exists only as computer code stored in a computer file. When running, a VM calls for resources from a hypervisor, of which there are two types. Both types get the resources that the VM requests.

A type 1 of hypervisor runs on the hardware; it is a full operating system. A type 1 hypervisor is not good for this application. A type 2 hypervisor is just a computer program, not a full operating system; it is perfect for this application. I am going to describe how to start running a VM to illustrate that most people can do it if they have to.

Here are the high points of how you could do it. Unless you are buying a Mac, be sure to opt for the Professional level of the Windows Operating System with at least 16 gigabytes of main memory and at least 500 GB of hard drive space. These attributes are not extreme; you might own them right now. In Windows 10, turn on Hyper-V; the internet will tell you how. After re-booting, you have a type 2 hypervisor named Hyper-V, on your machine. It will place nothing on your desktop, task bar, or start menu. Over time, Hyper-V may show on the start menu if you use it a lot. Usually, it does not show.

Start Hyper-V by clicking on "Start," typing, "hy" and starting Hyper-V. The internet will tell you all about creating virtual machines, networking them virtually to your network card, loading just about any operating system you want (which you might need to buy), and loading software on it. A virtual machine file (which constitutes the entirety of the VM) can reside on a USB stick; virtual machines are thus portable and concealable. For Christian studies, you could run Logos (from logos.com), which leaves only a little residue on your laptop.

You are there. But, do not forget, a computer forensics technician could still ferret out what you are doing.

Logos runs on a Mac, which has its own hypervisor called Hypervisor. You could construct the equivalent virtual machine and even mix operating systems.

You do not need continuous internet. You do need the internet to install Logos on your machine or a virtual machine. After that, you do not need the internet at all to read a book from your digital library, which was downloaded during installation.

I have only given the highlights, but I have shown you can function in secret. If you have a residence or other location where you can be sure to be the only one who views your computer screen, you are secure. Non-religious music and sports on the TV add more cover. You could even live dangerously near others who would be a threat, living out the 23rd Psalm, "Thou preparest a table before me in the presence of mine enemies."

An objection can be heard, "Aren't we required to publicly proclaim Christ and be baptized?" My response is that even Jesus taught that discretion is the better part of valor, "when they persecute you in this city, flee ye into another. "—Matthew 10:23.

Let's take the case of someone who, "as a tender plant, and as a root out of a dry ground," secretly becomes a Christian in the very midst of where it might be a punishable offence. This Christian has yet to be baptized. The baptism itself might be a death sentence. The quickest way to dispose of the theory that one must receive a sacrament to be saved is to bring forth the case of the crucified thief who was saved in Luke 23:32-43. He had no sacrament.

Is the spiritual life of an underground Christian deprived? Not hardly. Take for instance, my weekly reading of Luther. It was not in any way done in secret, but it could have been. It is richness to be taught by Luther and St. Augustine in the way I have described.

Hopefully, we will never need an Underground Church in America.

www.ingramcontent.com/pod-product-compliance
Lightning Source LLC
LaVergne TN
LVHW050553160826
845677LV00011B/2299

* 9 7 9 8 3 6 5 1 2 0 2 9 7 *